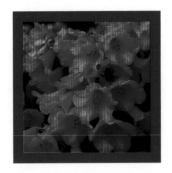

Pukeiti

NEW ZEALAND'S FINEST

RHODODENDRON GARDEN

Pukeiti

NEW ZEALAND'S FINEST RHODODENDRON GARDEN

Pat Greenfield

Pukeiti's Flora and Fauna by Graham Smith,
Director, Pukeiti Rhododendron Trust

David Bateman

First published in 1997 by
David Bateman Ltd, 30 Tarndale Grove, Albany Business Park,
Auckland, New Zealand

ISBN 1 86953 286 4

Design by Sue Reidy Design and Alchemy Design

Printed in Hong Kong by Colorcraft Ltd

Front cover, main photo: The spectacular circular bed just down from the lodge at Pukeiti. The vibrant pink rhododendron centre left is *R.* 'College Pink'.

Front cover, small photos from top: *R. magnificum* x *macabeanum*, *R.* 'Gilded Sunrise', *R. prostitum* var. *giganteum* 'Pukeiti', *R.* 'Lem's Cameo'.

Back cover: Pukeiti from the air, with the Pouakai Ranges brooding in the background.

Half title: *R.* 'Winsome'.

Opposite title page: *R.* 'Loder's White'.

Title page: *R.* 'Ernest Gill'.

Right: *R. grande*.

Opposite, from top: *R. javanicum* var *brookeanum*; *R.* 'Lem's Cameo'; *R.* 'Noyo Chief'.

Contents

Foreword

I first joined Pukeiti in 1955 while working as a student at Duncan & Davies. A year later, while I was gardening at Tupare, Pukeiti became a part of my life. Every Saturday I willingly crammed into an old Vauxhall car with Russell Matthews and set off 'up the hill'. This unlikely contribution to the 'working bee' at the fledgling garden would make rapid and sometimes spectacular progress up Carrington Road — potholes, blind corners and opposing traffic notwithstanding. Just getting to Pukeiti was an adventure in itself.

The overwhelming atmosphere in those days was the excitement of the project ahead and the wonderful camaraderie of the band of workers assembled. Mr Matthews would have spent many hours on the telephone encouraging, persuading and cajoling them to attend.

Pukeiti was scarcely a garden in 1956. Apart from the lodge and many hundreds of trees and shrubs lined out in nursery rows on the 'lawn', it consisted mainly of raw tracks straggling through the bush, fringed with newly planted rhododendrons. Possums were rife and frequently goats came down from the nearby Pouakai Ranges. Overnight they could ruin new plantings, but unwavering optimism prevailed.

Those early endeavours have brought about a garden of international importance — endeavours sustained over the years by many dedicated volunteers and staff alike. It is remarkable that in all this time there have been only five curators. Pukeiti is now known all over the world as a unique temperate rainforest garden.

Earlier visionaries dreamed too that one day the Pukeiti story would be recorded in words and pictures in book form. Pat Greenfield has achieved this with remarkable style, bringing the early days to life and faithfully recording the later years. Pat has made an invaluable contribution to the fabric of the Pukeiti Rhododendron Trust. I know visitors, members and friends of Pukeiti alike will find this a fascinating book, and I am looking forward to receiving my copy.

Gordon Collier
Titoki Point

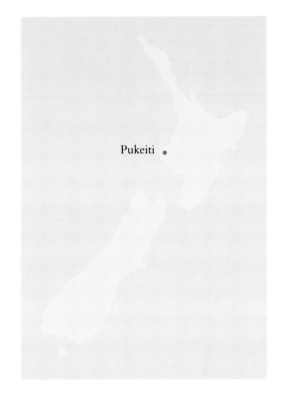

Pukeiti

Opposite: Part of the Rowe Walk on a brilliantly fine day. The pink rhododendron in the left foreground is R. 'Merle Lee'.

Preface

This book really began with my late companion Les who was crippled with arthritis. Being unable to work full time, I honed my writing and photographic skills. This lead to my writing and photographing for gardening magazines and a calendar. Les accompanied me on my outings for research, which provided social sustenance for us both. This was back in 1990 when we lived in Auckland.

After my mother passed away, we moved to New Plymouth where my brother lived. Once there, we took advantage of Taranaki's many beautiful gardens. Pukeiti in particular entranced us both with its magnificent rhododendrons and abundant birdlife.

Les passed away in 1993, and after a painful period of grieving, I decided to do something positive — perhaps write a book. I thought about Pukeiti. Both Mum and Les have been there and I had happy memories of them in this wonderful place.

I was soon to discover that embarking on such a book was not akin to writing a giant gardening article. Progress was slow and difficult. I was confident of my photographic and research skills, but less so of my ability to convey Pukeiti's essence through the written word. Encouragement from the people at Pukeiti and others helped me through the rough patches. I discovered that above all Pukeiti is about people; their struggles, set backs and triumphs. Despite all, they persevered and delivered a lasting reward in the magnificence of the Pukeiti Rhododendron Trust garden.

I would also like to acknowledge here the work of the Director of Pukeiti, Graham Smith, in providing the chapters on the botanical collections and other flora and fauna of Pukeiti.

Pat Greenfield
New Plymouth

Opposite: Pukeiti Stream.

Acknowledgements

I wish to convey my gratitude to the following people for the invaluable assistance they have given me on Pukeiti and its history: Graham Smith, Lady Mary Matthews, Richard Matthews, John Matthews, John (Jack) Goodwin, Elsie King, Des Corbett, Keith Adams, Gordon Collier, Garry Clapperton of Eastwoodhill, and the New Zealand Rhododendron Association. Also to Tracey Borgfeldt and Joy Browne for their professional assistance. Finally to others who, knowingly or unknowingly, have contributed in the compilation of this book. To all of you go my heartfelt thanks.

Technical notes

A Pentax 6 x 7 medium format camera was used for the photography in this book (excluding the historical photos). They were shot from my entire range of lenses, comprising 55 mm through to 300 mm. In most instances a tripod was used. Fujichrome Provia 100 was my main film. All of the photographs were taken in available light, and no filters were used.

CHAPTER ONE

The founding of the garden

At first glance, the killing fields of Gallipoli and the Somme would appear to have nothing in common with Pukeiti. In a paradox of history, however, one gave birth to the other.

War can bring out the beast in man, but it can also bring out the best. After two world wars and the decimation of many parts of the Old World, and not a few areas of New Zealand, there seemed to be a general coming together of people interested in plants. The ravages of war and its lost generations, combined with the blackened stumps of a blighted local landscape cleared for pasture, made some people aware of what was being destroyed. Trees, flowers and birds, amongst other things, 'restoreth the soul'. If all this and the freedom to enjoy them were lost, then the futility of war would have been complete.

Farsighted people saw the urgent need to put something back, and preserve some of the land before it disappeared forever. New organisations for various horticultural purposes were set up, both nationally and internationally. These would not only promote the growing of flowering plants, but would also generally enhance and preserve the environment. The New Zealand Rhododendron Association was one such organisation. The initiative for its founding was a suggestion by Professor (later Sir Geoffrey) Peren, then principal of Massey Agricultural College. In the early 1940s, Massey had a committee called variously 'the college arboretum committee' or 'the horticultural committee', members being Professor Peren, Dame Elizabeth Knox-Gilmer, Mr W.D. Cook, Mr (later Sir Victor) Davies, Mr P. Black and Dr John S. Yeates.

Following Professor Peren's suggestion, a meeting of this committee, together with Dr C. King, was held on the evening of 10 August 1944. It was decided that a New Zealand Rhododendron Association (NZRA) be formed by those present. The formal application for incorporation was signed by the following foundation members: E.F. Stead, Mrs E.M. Knox-Gilmer, T.E.Y. Seddon, W.D. Cook, J. Edmondston, C. King, P. Black, D.C. Mackenzie, F.J.E. Jollie, T.L. Penn, Mrs M.E. Burrell, V.C. Davies, R. Cook, G.S. Peren and J.S. Yeates.

On 6 September 1944, a circular letter was sent out to some enthusiasts who were considered likely to be interested in joining. It stated in part:

The objects of the Association are:
a. To act as a common meeting ground for rhododendron enthusiasts.
b. To encourage the cultivation, the study, and the improvement of rhododendrons by such means as the Association shall see fit.

It is hoped to arrange to have the annual meeting each year during October, changing the place of the meeting each year so that members may visit the main rhododendron growing centres year by year during the flowering season.

At the first annual general meeting, held at Massey College on 4 October 1944, and attended by some 50 people, Mr Edgar Stead was elected President, Professor G.S. Peren Chairman and Dr J.S. Yeates Secretary-Treasurer. A council consisting of Mrs E. Knox-Gilmer and Messrs P. Black, W.D. Cook, V.C. Davies and T.L. Penn was elected unopposed, and the NZRA was under way.

Overseas authorities on rhododendrons were agreed that New Zealand was one of the best places in the world in which to grow these beautiful plants. J.G. Millais, in his book *Rhododendrons and the various hybrids*, published in 1924, had stated that 'the North Island of New Zealand is especially suitable for rhododendrons, and splendid gardens of these plants could be formed there'.

Above: The Stead Walk leading to the Hybrid Block features 'Loderi' rhododendrons, New Zealand-raised hybrids, camellias and hydrangeas. Pukeiti

Opposite: The dam and spillway on Pukeiti Stream.

NZRA foundation member William Douglas Cook was known to have had a dream of a vast national garden of rhododendrons, planted against the background of our own beautiful native bush. Prior to World War I, Douglas drew the ballot for sections 1 and 2 at the Ngatapa Estate near Gisborne. He named his new property Eastwoodhill, after the part of Thornliebank, Scotland, where his mother's family lived. Eastwoodhill was cleared from virgin manuka, then Douglas bought more land and stocked it all with sheep, before turning his thoughts to planting trees for shelter and other plants.

Douglas was called up in 1914. In World War 1 he served in the Light Artillery in Egypt, then at Gallipoli and lastly in France. He lost the end of a finger to a bullet in Gallipoli, and the sight of one eye at the Somme in France. While recuperating with family in Scotland, he came to admire the lovely gardens and homes there. This was the impetus for him to begin planning a garden at Eastwoodhill, and ultimately Pukeiti.

He realised that while he could never have the home or the lifestyle enjoyed by the Scottish relatives, he could have the garden. In his own words, 'I'd got the idea, after staying with wealthy relatives and their friends, that I too could have lovely surroundings, even if I could never have a fine home and live as they did. That was the start of the park. A dignified park to drive through to my home — whatever its size. Set your heart on an objective and believe in your heart you'll achieve it and you will. Where most men fail is in lack of faith in themselves.'[1]

When Douglas returned to Eastwoodhill, he planted some of the many trees then available in New Zealand, including oregons, chestnuts and oaks. He searched the country for new species and varieties, and eventually travelled overseas where he visited the world's most famous gardens, making notes on the plants that appealed to him. Though interested mainly in trees and shrubs, he also planted many unusual perennials and bulbs.

Douglas began to import plants not available here. During the Depression he concentrated on building up an extensive collection of many interesting plant genera, including maples, cherries and magnolias. Over the ensuing years, Eastwoodhill grew from around 620 acres (250 hectares) to about 1250 acres (500 hectares). As well as channelling profits from the farm into the plantings, Douglas also mortgaged the farm many times to raise money. He was later quoted as saying, 'I never was a farmer. That was only a means of living in the country and being my own boss. I never could stand taking orders and loved roaming the hills.'[2]

Right: The water-wheel on Pukeiti Stream was installed in 1957 and generated power for two years until mains power came to Pukeiti. Since then, it has been used to provide water to buildings and for irrigation.

Bottom left: Mt Taranaki seen from the North Egmont Visitors Centre side.

Bottom right: A tree fern standing against a rain-saturated sky on the Brewster Walk. (In 1995 almost 4.8 metres of rain fell, the most ever recorded at Pukeiti.)

In the early 1950s, Douglas sold 980 acres (395 hectares) of the farm in order to raise more funds. He planted 65 hectares of the remaining land in what must be the most comprehensive collection of exotic trees ever established in New Zealand. This effectively became known as the Eastwoodhill Arboretum.

The search for a suitable property

To fulfil his earlier dream of a vast natural garden of rhododendrons — he couldn't grow them successfully at Eastwoodhill because of its unsuitable soils and dry climate — Douglas interested a number of enthusiasts, including Russell Matthews, in his scheme, and enlisted their cooperation in finding the right property. He himself had been searching for six or eight years for such a place in Taranaki. Russell Matthews had searched further afield. Some land looked at seemed ideal for rhododendron cultivation, but was too far away from civilisation to be a desirable site for a rhododendron park.

By 1950, the group of enthusiasts had all but given up hope of finding such a place. In autumn of that year Douglas drove over to New Plymouth, planning to attend the NZRA Council's meeting due to be held at Massey on 9 March. They were to discuss the proposal of acquiring land to build up a rhododendron collection, with perhaps one such area in each island. This roughly fitted in with Douglas's line of thinking. All he and the others needed now was a change of luck.

Whilst imbibing at the Criterion Hotel, Russell and Douglas had a convivial conversation with MP Ernie Aderman and Arthur Goudie, among others. When the subject of land came up Mr Aderman suggested they try the Upper Carrington Road in New Plymouth. Up there was a block of bush which he thought would be ideal for their purpose and was for sale.

Douglas Cook and Russell Matthews set out shortly afterwards to inspect the area. The 153-and-a-half acre (63 hectare) block of bush was on a hill called Pukeiti. As Douglas walked through the bush, he was entranced by its lushness and the filmy ferns. The magnificent view, which encompassed 100 to 150 kilometres up the surfbound coast, over all north Taranaki and away to Mt Ruapehu, also took his breath away. Rhododendrons planted nearby looked clean and healthy, even though grown in a neglected old garden.

Douglas had a singleness of purpose and drive — almost an impatience — to get things done. 'One walk through was enough,' he said. 'I knew I'd found the right spot. That night I located the owner and bought it.'[3] He was later perturbed because he had pre-empted the NZRA meeting, due to be held the following day.

Top: The Gatehouse, opened in 1987, and summer borders. Pukeiti

Above left: R. scabridibracteum, *collected on Mt Gahavisukar in Papua New Guinea. Many of Pukeiti's Vireya rhododendrons have been sourced from the highlands of Papua New Guinea.* Pukeiti

Above right: The West Irian form of R. konori, *collected from the western (Indonesian) half of New Guinea.* Pukeiti

Douglas's first idea had been to develop the land himself and hand it over to the NZRA upon his death. Upon giving himself time to reflect, he realised that would have meant neglecting Eastwoodhill, his life's work. After careful deliberation, he decided to offer the land to the Association if it was in a financial position to develop it as a rhododendron park. His proposal was put forward at the annual conference held at Massey Agricultural College on 25 October 1950.

The Association declined Douglas's offer for a number of reasons, the main one being a lack of financial resources. (Land offered by H.J. Marchant was also turned down.) Another was because they were not sure that Douglas's vision of a rhododendron park would be successful, and if not, they didn't want to be associated with a failure. Setting up such a park was a big undertaking in those days, and hadn't been tried before. Personalities too played a key role, and 'under the table' views were not usually put down on paper. Heated

exchanges are a part and parcel of many momentous meetings and events. Often they determine the outcome, successful or otherwise, of whatever proposal had been put forward. Douglas Cook's offer was no exception.

The proposed objectives of Pukeiti's developers differed from those of the NZRA quite markedly. Pukeiti was put forward as a park, open to a widely spread, large membership, whereas the Association preferred to remain a smaller group, comprised of the keener and more specialised rhododendron growers. (Pukeiti's climate range was also seen as being too narrow.) Some Association members were opposed to the idea outright, perhaps none more so than Dr Yeates, the Secretary-Treasurer, who perceived a splitting of funds. In addition, he and Russell Matthews just didn't get on. Because of Dr Yeates's position, his views carried a lot of sway and Pukeiti was turned down. (For a number of years, Pukeiti and the NZRA were never of a like mind, except that some members belonged to both. Some members of each group were opposed to the other. Happily today this is not the case.)

Undeterred, Douglas offered to donate the land to a group of keen NZRA members and others, providing that not less than 20 persons joined up. A trust was to be established and each member would have to be prepared to subscribe £50 a year for a minimum period of five years. This was to provide a substantial nucleus of membership for the Trust to carry out its objectives. Russell Matthews spearheaded the drive for sustaining members and others, canvassing in both the North and South Islands of New Zealand.

The Trust is formed

On 28 September 1951, 22 people signed an application for registration for a Certificate of Incorporation. They were in the order of signing: M.G. Maxwell, V.C. Davies, G.W.A. Williams, P.J. Ayckbourn, M.R. Brewster, A.L. Richardson, A.H. Goudie, R. Matthews, C.H. Croker, J.M. Hudson, E.M. Matthews, R.K. Ireland, F.A. Ireland, K.B. Burns, R.F. Stead, T.H.N. White, A.C. Kynoch, A.G. Larcom, R.C. Gordon, A.H. Marshall, W.D. Cook, H.N. Rowe.

On 25 October 1951, a Certificate of Incorporation No. T.1951/13 stated that the Pukeiti Rhododendron Trust Incorporated was now a legal fact. The objects of the society were given as:

a. To act as a common meeting ground for Rhododendron and Horticultural enthusiasts.

b. To promote interest in the genus *Rhododendron*, scientific research in its breeding and culture: standardisation of its varietal names, the dissemination of information concerning the above and promotion of such other purposes as may advance the culture of

Rhododendrons and other trees, shrubs and plants of every description.

    c. To beautify the whole of the land acquired.

    d. To provide sanctuary for all bird life.

    e. With a view to the better carrying out of the aforesaid objects to acquire freehold or leasehold lands and in particular to acquire from the owner thereof all that piece of freehold land containing 153 acres 2 roods, more or less being Sec 2 Blk V11 Cape S.D. and to develop the same as a Rhododendron and General Botanical trial ground and Park. [Today this is known as the Cook Block.]

In conjunction with this, provision was also made for other types of membership.

A circular notice was sent out to local members on the day after, advising them of Pukeiti's official opening due the following week. This was timed to coincide with the NZRA's Annual Conference, being held in New Plymouth from 30 October to 1 November. Members of the Association were invited to visit Pukeiti on Wednesday, 31 October, weather permitting.

The Inaugural Annual General Meeting of the Pukeiti Rhododendron Trust (Inc) was held at the Devon Dining Rooms, Devon Street, New Plymouth, on Wednesday 31 October 1951 at 8 pm. From the minutes we see that during this meeting Russell Matthews outlined the preliminary history of the Trust, stemming from the magnificent offer of 153 acres (62 hectares) of land by Mr W.D. Cook of Gisborne. Arthur Goudie reported on the development work completed to date in preparation for planting. The acquisition of rhododendrons and preservation of the native bush was also discussed.

The initial meeting of the Board of the Trust was held at the conclusion of the Inaugural AGM at 11 pm. The following is an extract from the minutes of that meeting:

Present: Messrs W.D. Cook, Roland Stead, J.M. Hudson, Russell Cook, J.F. Brown (Members): and also the following as co-opted members: Messrs Russell Matthews, A.H. Goudie, J.W. Goodwin, C.H. Croker, G.W. Williams, A.L. Richardson and M.G. Maxwell.
Chairman: Mr W.D. Cook was appointed Chairman, and Mr G.W. Williams Deputy Chairman.
Secretary: Mr G.J. Broker, Public Accountant of Patea, was appointed Secretary.
Local Executive: The following were elected as Local Executive: Messrs G.W. Williams, Russell Matthews, M.G. Maxwell, A.H. Goudie, A.L. Richardson, J.W. Goodwin, Douglas Elliott (Croker/Russell Cook).

Honorary Curator: Mr A.H. Goudie was appointed Honorary Curator at an honorarium of £50 p.a. (Matthews/Richardson).
Bank Account: It was resolved that a current account be kept at the Australia and New Zealand Bank Limited, and that any two of Messrs Russell Matthews, A.H. Goudie and G.J. Broker be and are hereby authorised to operate the said account.
Publicity: Mr J.F. Brown was appointed to report the initial meeting for the press, in cooperation with Mr A.H. Goudie.
Membership Drive: The draft copy for the brochure prepared free of charge by Messrs Inglis Wright Ltd was referred to the Local Executive.
Delegation of Powers: On the motion of Mr R.K. Ireland, seconded by Mr W.D. Cook, it was decided that all the powers of the Board be delegated to the Local Executive in the meantime, pending a further meeting of the Board to be called in approximately six months' time.

The meeting concluded at about midnight.

The official opening of Pukeiti took place on Thursday, 1 November 1951. This was held at what was later known as the Cook Entrance, which leads up to Pukeiti Hill. About 40 members and visitors made the journey. A bus conveyed 24 from the post office, and on its arrival half a dozen cars were also found to be there. John (Jack) Goodwin remembered it well. 'They'd shifted up some plants to give the place a rhodo appearance on that first day. When we arrived in the car, there wasn't a leaf left. Two goats had taken a shine to them!'[4] (John Goodwin was the Superintendent of Parks for New Plymouth. From 1953 to 1968 he acted as Honorary Superintendent to Pukeiti, giving it invaluable advice and unassuming assistance.)

Douglas Cook, donor of the Trust property, cut a ribbon and officially opened the gates. The visitors walked from the shack right through to the summit, along the partly formed road and through the bush track. All were amazed at the volume of work already done, and the beauty of the native bush. Sadly, mist gave way to rain, denying a view from any part of the track. However, although many coats and shoes were soaked with the downpour, no one was disappointed. One member later remarked, 'In what other field but horticulture could you run such a trip so successfully in the pouring rain?'

Upon returning to the bus, seven new members were enrolled. One member also donated anonymously the cost of the bus hire. During the welcome cup of tea where everything was dampened but their spirits, some must have wondered what they would be seeing there if they lived for another 20 years.

Philip John Ayckbourn

Monica Romaine Brewster

Kenneth Bickerton Burns

The Foundation Members

As at 1 November 1951, there were 25 Foundation (Sustaining) Members. The following information and photographs (where known and where available), will give a brief insight into the varied backgrounds of those original supporters of Pukeiti.

Philip John Ayckbourn

Born in the UK in 1901. Died in 1955.

Philip Ayckbourn went to Birmingham University at age 16, taking a science degree in metallurgy. He sailed for New Zealand on the *Tainui* during the 1920s. Here he worked for Kempthorne Prosser before joining his father, who had founded the Cambrian Engineering Works. Philip enjoyed music and gardening, the latter prompting his interest in the concept of Pukeiti. His wife continued to support Pukeiti after his death at the early age of 54.

Monica Romaine Brewster (née Govett)

Born in New Plymouth in 1886. Died in 1973.

Monica Govett went to the UK prior to World War I with her mother and sister. She later returned to New Zealand on board the *Kagoma* where she met Dr Rex Brewster Snr, the medical officer on board. They were married in 1922, then moved overseas again prior to World War II, where they lived for a time in Vienna.

Monica was one of New Plymouth's great benefactors. One gift resulted in the Govett-Brewster Art Gallery. Her great interest in gardens led to her becoming a Foundation Member. The Brewster Walk was named in her honour.

Kenneth Bickerton Burns

Born in Christchurch 25 July 1891. Died in 1975.

Ken Burns left school at age 12 and went to work on a cattle station in Gisborne. Enlisting in 1915, he went to France with the Canterbury Regiment. He was later awarded the Distinguished Conduct Medal.

Ken married Francis Bowler in 1922 and purchased Mount Ross Station near Middlemarch in 1924. Six years later Francis became ill and was not expected to recover. Her husband thoughtfully planted roses, peonies, delphiniums and other plants so that she would have an attractive scene to look at from her bedroom window. It was out of this family tragedy that Ken's love of plants was born. He bought Otiritiri in Timaru in 1938, and lived there until 1963. At Otiritiri he developed his love of rare plants, creating a gardener's paradise. The property is now the Gleniti Golf Club.

Ken was elected a member of the NZRA in 1948. He was known as 'K.B.' to his many horticultural friends. In 1965 he was made an Associate of Honour of the Royal New Zealand Institute of Horticulture (RNZIH), for distinguished services.

William Douglas Cook (Founder of Pukeiti)

Born in New Plymouth 28 October 1884. Died 27 April 1967.

The son of a banker, Douglas Cook lived with his parents in many parts of New Zealand. He was particularly enthralled by Mt Egmont (Mt Taranaki) and the luxuriance of its tree ferns.

After being educated, presumably at Auckland, Douglas spent his early years working on several farms in the Hawke's Bay region. In 1910 he landed by surfboat and journeyed inland to the hill country beyond Ngatapa, Gisborne. Here Douglas established his farm, Eastwoodhill.

Douglas served during World War I and was lucky to survive campaigns at both Gallipoli and France. After returning to Eastwoodhill, he steadily built it up to a pre-eminent place in New Zealand horticulture. He married Claire Bourne on 20 October 1930.

William Douglas Cook

The 'Cold War' and its threat of destruction of the gardens of Europe gave Douglas impetus to use Eastwoodhill as a repository for good plant material. He was sure that Europe would be blown apart. After such a war, people would be able to come to him and collect material to start new gardens.

Douglas Cook was one of New Zealand's most knowledgeable plantsmen. He was an early member of the RNZIH and was made a Fellow of the same on 17 February 1948. On 17 February 1966 he was elected an Associate of Honour to that body — the highest New Zealand award. He was a Foundation Member of the International Dendrology Society and of the NZRA. For many years Douglas was a Fellow of the Royal Horticultural Society (RHS) in Great Britain. In 1965, on the recommendation of John Goodwin, the RHS honoured his services to horticulture with the Veitch Memorial Gold Medal.

Inez Rachael May Corrigan

In the personal arena, Douglas was seen as a complex, sometimes strange man, with a number of foibles. He was also a perfectionist who valued tradition. For example, he liked occasions which called for a formal English dinner to be done properly — to him it was important how far you put your plates in and the way in which you separated the cutlery, even down to the details such as the crease in your tablecloth.

During the 1960s when his money ran out, Douglas was desperate to find someone to succeed him at Eastwoodhill. Eventually a Mr H.B. Williams was approached and he offered to buy the arboretum at government valuation. Douglas was thrilled, as he knew Eastwoodhill would not be harmed under Bill Williams's stewardship. His greatest fear had been of a neighbouring farmer purchasing it and putting cattle through his plantings.

Douglas loved rhododendrons and despite some disappointments along the way, Pukeiti fulfilled his dream of growing them to perfection. (He was made its Patron in 1952.) Unfortunately, this man of unusual vision did not live to see the completion of the Summit Drive Lookout. However, along with other early members, he received great satisfaction from the opening of bush walks, access to streams and the water-wheel. Today, both Pukeiti and Eastwoodhill are preserved for the nation.

Inez Rachael May Corrigan (née Purser)

Born in Hawera 11 November 1897. Died 4 May 1970.

Educated at the Hawera Convent, Inez studied music under Sister Charles, and played both cello and the piano. During World War I she toured Taranaki with the Bing Boys, organised by Mr Terry Gormley, to raise funds to assist soldiers returning from the war. This 'Belgian Fund', as it was known throughout New Zealand, formed the basis of funds for the formation of the Returned Services' Association. For 30 years after the war, Inez was one of a group who provided concerts in the South Taranaki RSA Clubrooms after ANZAC parades.

Cyril Henry Croker

Victor C. Davies

Ronald Claris Gordon

In 1923, Inez married Alexander James Corrigan in Hawera. He was known throughout New Zealand for his interest in sheepdog trialling, developing unpromising land, and trotting. In 1936, the couple built a new home, Parkhill, on an undeveloped site on the South Road west of Hawera. It was designed by Mr Raymond Syme, who also later designed Pukeiti's lodge. Inez engaged Mr Francis Morshead of New Plymouth to landscape the approximately 2 acres (0.8 hectares) of garden. Her association with him heightened her interest in gardening, and ultimately led to her becoming a Foundation Member. (She paid for this out of her own money, not that of her husband.)

Cyril Henry Croker

Born in Christchurch 27 March 1888. Died in 1958.

Cyril Croker's family moved around the South Island wherever his father was manager for the NZ Loan Mercantile Company. He completed his education at Otago University and later settled in New Plymouth where he practised law until his death. He was a very keen gardener and a strong advocate for Pukeiti. He chaired the inaugural meeting which resolved to form the Pukeiti Rhododendron Trust. Cyril's other leisure interests included athletics, cross-country running and tennis.

Victor C. Davies (Later Sir Victor Davies)

Born in New Plymouth in 1887. Died in 1977.

Victor Davies was apprenticed to a nurseryman, J.R. Duncan, in 1902. A few years after completing his apprenticeship, the firm of Duncan & Davies was formed — and this involvement occupied the rest of his working life. During this time, the firm grew from an original half-acre nursery to become the largest producer of ornamental trees and shrubs in the Southern Hemisphere. Many plants were donated by 'V.C.' from the nursery to get Pukeiti going — a practice that has continued to the present day.

Ronald Claris Gordon

Born in Taihape in 1916.

Ron and his twin brother Ian were interested in gardening from an early age, encouraged by their mother, who taught them the names of plants and took them to flower shows.(Ron, however, was more interested in the coconut ice!) After completing his education, Ron worked on the family farm near Taihape.

Ron left for America and Europe in 1938 and was managing his brother-in-law's farm on the Isle of Islay when war broke out. Returning home in 1941, he joined the Air Force, training in Canada as navigator under the Empire Air Training Scheme. He elected to serve in England and was attached to the RAF, Squadrons 101, 460 and 625. In 1942 he received the DFM and in 1945 was awarded the DFC, being demobilised on VE Day.

Returning home, Ron bought his farm at Rongoiti in 1947. In 1962 he married Helen Collier. They subsequently had three sons.

Ron's first interest in trees was for erosion control, later for general planting. He had a special interest in conifers, but also focussed on winter colour and plantings for birds. Ron joined the NZRA in 1949, and in 1951 became one of Pukeiti's Foundation Members. In due course he was elected to the Board, later holding the position of Chairman for a period of six years. He was made Patron of Pukeiti in 1992.

Ron has made many horticultural trips abroad, including visits to the UK in 1972, Nepal in 1976 and Sikkim in 1978. He helped to cement closer ties between Pukeiti and the Kunming Botanical Institute in

Yunnan, China, having travelled to that country in 1981, 1984, 1987, 1990 and 1992. His garden at Rongoiti reflects a lifelong interest in horticulture, and his knowledge of plants is encyclopaedic. He is also an accomplished plant breeder, having created the highly acclaimed *Rhododendron* 'Rubicon'.

Arthur Harold Goudie

Born in Rotorua in 1905. Died in 1975.

Arthur Harold Goudie

Arthur's father, Halbert Alexander Goudie, served with the State Forest Service for 25 years, rising to the position of Conservator of Forests. He resigned in 1926 to start his own nursery in Rotorua, growing trees and shrubs. With this background, it is not surprising that upon completing his formal education, the young Arthur chose a career in horticulture. He took up employment with Duncan & Davies, and it was here that he met Maude Prestige, a fellow employee who later became his wife and lifelong companion. Arthur stayed with this firm until about 1930, when he left to start up his own nursery in New Plymouth.

Sylvan Nurseries, as it was known, specialised in trees and shrubs, with an emphasis on rhododendrons. Later, *Lilium auratum* and its hybrids became a specialty of the nursery. Arthur was a plantsman. He read widely on horticulture, and corresponded with many overseas nurserymen and authors of plant books. He was always interested in new plants. Among the many introductions he made *Cotinus coggygria (Rhus cotinus)* and *Rhododendron yakushimanum* stand out.

As a boy, Arthur won a battle with poliomyelitis, but during the late forties his health prevented him from doing physical work and he returned to Duncan & Davies as assistant manager. It was at this time that he became involved with others in the concept of a park dedicated to rhododendrons. For climatic reasons Taranaki was an obvious choice. After the Pukeiti site was acquired Arthur became one of the 25 Foundation Members and its first curator (1951-3). In 1954 he took a position as general manager with Harrisons' Nurseries in Palmerston North. Arthur retired in 1970, but continued his horticultural involvement as a consultant and adviser to various nurseries and park departments until his death.

John Michael Hudson

Born at Gwavas, Hawke's Bay, 25 September 1930.

John Michael Hudson

After leaving school, Michael Hudson worked on a number of farms. He then attended the Massey Agricultural College where he gained a Diploma in Agriculture with a sheep option. After a few years away, Michael returned home to manage the family farm. He represents the sixth generation of family ownership of Gwavas since 1857, when Major George Gwavas Carlyon bought the property of 12,500 hectares. The estate, now consisting of about 1100 hectares, lies at around 300 metres above sea level, and enjoys some 100 centimetres of rain annually.

Trees are a great feature of Gwavas. There are 120 hectares of podocarp bush preserved since 1858, and a wealth of mature exotic trees, many over 100 years old. The garden was laid out by Major Carlyon's son in the 1880s, in the style of Cornish woodland estates. The oldest trees, planted by 1860, include a *Pinus radiata* and an oak. It is a woodland garden on a grand scale, with the pine, fir and larch canopy thrusting 30 metres above the ground. Underneath, a host of choice shrubs abound, including rhododendrons, magnolias and many rare ornamental plants.

With this great family tradition, it was inevitable that Michael would develop an interest in gardening. He was a member of the NZRA from 1957 to 1977. Today Michael still maintains an avid interest in his woodland garden, and is considered to be one of New Zealand's leading tree and shrub experts.

*Freda Agnes Ireland and
Robert Kay Ireland*

Andrew Gale Larcom

Freda Agnes Ireland (née Blythe) and Robert Kay Ireland

Freda Agnes Ireland born 22 May 1891. Died 8 December 1965.

Robert Kay Ireland born 20 December 1882. Died 4 March 1960.

Mr and Mrs Ireland were both born in Oamaru. They married in 1915. Robert Ireland's father, John Ireland, emigrated to Dunedin from Scotland in 1858, settling in Oamaru where he partnered the establishment of a small flourmill. Robert was born in 1882 and educated in Oamaru. When his father died in 1910, Robert took on the running of the mill during a period of intense competition. He succeeded to the point of acquiring one of the largest milling companies in New Zealand, and just before he died was building a new mill at Mt Maunganui.

In 1922, Robert acquired Ribbonwood, a South Canterbury high country sheep station which he immediately proceeded to develop, introducing techniques then not normally used in the Mackenzie Country. These included very extensive irrigation, high quality pasture and fodder cropping. He established a Merino stud based on Haddon Rig and Boonoke stock, also an Aberdeen Angus stud based on stock which he imported from Scotland. To facilitate these, he acquired farming units at Waitaki and Oamaru. Other business activities included involvement in a Malaysian rubber plantation and importation of petrol from America. Robert Ireland also chaired the local harbour board and was a town councillor.

Freda Ireland was very active in church and social affairs. These interests quickly extended to moral support of her husband in commercial matters, becoming chairperson of the Ireland companies for two years after his death.

With her husband, she became involved in horticulture in the 1920s. They developed the property known as Waianakarua, named after the river which flows through it. Robert had purchased the south Oamaru property prior to their marriage with the intention of re-establishing indigenous New Zealand flora. This they proceeded to do together, and due to the presence of water on the property, they were able to ride out the notorious Otago droughts.

Freda's early interests were in daffodils and roses which she exhibited at several gatherings in New Zealand; Robert's involvement was mainly in native and exotic trees. After a while they focussed on rhododendrons, with encouragement from Edgar Stead. Their enthusiasm became well known and they gladly accepted the invitation to assist in the founding of Pukeiti.

Ada Clements Kynoch (Mrs)

Born in 1908. Died November 1996.

Ada married Oswald Evelyn Kynoch in about 1930. Oswald, born in Scotland on 5 July 1905, came out to New Zealand at the age of 19 and took up farming. In 1928, he purchased a property in Ashley Clinton, central Hawke's Bay, where he lived until his death on 13 July 1989. The farm and garden was named Kynachan, and even though both loved the countryside, the garden was Ada's domain and one of her great passions. Originally of about 0.6 hectares, it was expanded to over a hectare when a new house was built. Russell Cook (no relation to Douglas Cook), taught Ada a lot about plants, and her personal favourites were rhododendrons, camellias and maples.

It was through the enthusiasm of one of her gardening friends, Russell Matthews, that Ada Kynoch became a Foundation Member of Pukeiti. Her husband Oswald paid for her membership.

Andrew Gale Larcom

Born in Australia 2 February 1870. Died — unknown.

Andrew Larcom came to New Zealand in 1871. A pioneer farmer at Ararata, where he ran sheep and cattle, Andrew served on a variety of committees and boards and was also a director of the Farmers' Co-operative Association. He became interested in Pukeiti through his association with Griffith Williams.

Alan Hadfield Marshall

Born in 1900. Died in 1956.

Alan Hadfield Marshall

The Ridges garden in Marton was developed by Alan and May Marshall after they were married in 1924. It was to become the love of their life. Today, this famous garden, which has been featured on New Zealand television, is in the care of their granddaughter, Sally Spencer.

In 1946, Alfred Buxton was employed to design a number of extensions. During the early fifties, the sunken garden, walled with brick and featuring the now well known statue of Spring, which came from Crowther's in London, was established. A feature of The Ridges garden has always been its rhododendrons. This led to May and Alan's keen interest in the development of Pukeiti, and they made many trips to see it.

On the Marshall's farm, named Tutu Totara, special areas of native bush have been preserved, some of which are covenanted to the QE II National Trust.

Russell Matthews (Later Sir Russell Matthews, OBE)

Born in New Plymouth in 1896. Died in 1987.

Russell Mathews

A study of the Matthews family is included in Chapter 3, so the relevant information pertaining to Sir Russell is covered there.

Elizabeth Mary Matthews (née Brodie)

Born in Te Aroha in 1911.

Lady Matthews was educated at both the New Plymouth Girls' High School and Queen Margaret's College. See further information in Chapter 3.

Elizabeth Mary Matthews

Max Grant Maxwell

Arthur Louis Richardson

Max Grant Maxwell

Born in 1900. Died in 1986.

Grant Maxwell moved from his father's first property in Oaonui to a very swampy and much larger property in the same district in 1903. He only received a few months' secondary education at the New Plymouth Technical College as he had to run the family farm as his father was involved in a car accident. Grant, then 15, was assisted by his 13-year-old brother.

The property was a model farm and Grant was an innovative farmer. He had hopes of following an engineering career, especially in bridge architecture. He was also a keen photographer, making his own box cameras and developing his own film. In 1937 he married Dorothy Nora Berry. He was a self-taught botanist and silviculturist; his interest in New Zealand natives was such that at one stage he had one of the largest collections in the country. He was nominated for the coveted Loder Cup for horticulture in the 1950s.

Grant Maxwell was one of the instigators of farm forestry and the New Zealand Forestry Service. He oversaw and organised the planting of Perpetual Forest on the slopes of the Kaitake Ranges by Oakura, New Plymouth. He belonged to a number of organisations, including the Red Cross. He was a supporter of the Rahotu Anglican Church and was a Justice of the Peace. He also served on the board of Pukekura Park for many years. Pukeiti become an interest via Russell Matthews and others, and he became so enthusiastic about Pukeiti that he made all his family and six grandchildren 'Members in Perpetuity'.

Graham B. Pettison

Last known to have been living in Nelson.

Graham worked at Eastwoodhill for a time, and was later a plant propagator at Massey College. Douglas Cook wanted Graham to work at Pukeiti under the supervision of Arthur Goudie, but he preferred to 'do his own thing'. A skilled plantsman, Graham ultimately achieved his goal of owning a plant nursery.

Arthur Louis Richardson

Born in Ngaere, Taranaki, in 1886. Died in 1964.

Arthur Richardson attended his local school before starting work in the Mangorei Dairy Factory. He later successfully applied for the position of assistant manager and chief buttermaker at the Oakura Dairy Factory. While at Oakura, the call of the forest was strong. He spent much of his off-duty time walking through the Kaitake Ranges.

While working for the Okato Dairy Company, Arthur was married. Soon after, the decision was made to go into farming. He and his wife Ellen purchased a farm on Pitone Road, Okato, and this is where he spent the rest of his life. During his time on the farm, Arthur served on the local dairy factory board of directors for 15 years, and contributed generously to all local causes.

When the plan for Pukeiti was put forward, Arthur was very enthusiastic about it. He saw it as a way that he could spend his time in the bush again during his retirement from the farm.

Henry Nathaniel Rowe

Born in Bell Block, New Plymouth, in June 1885. Died in October 1973.

Henry Rowe's parents were farmers. He spent his early years working in dairy factories where along the way he learnt the building trade. Henry eventually went to work for Mr C.A. Wilkinson at his hardware shop in Eltham and later purchased this merchant's hardware store in New Plymouth.

Henry enjoyed gardening and landscaping. He became interested in Pukeiti through his association with Griffith Williams, spending many weeks up there on the tractor or bulldozer.

Henry Nathaniel Rowe

Roland Fraser Stead

Born at Ilam, Christchurch, in 1922.

Ilam was the rhododendron garden that Roland's father, Edgar, developed. Edgar Stead pioneered the growing of rhododendrons in New Zealand, and his 'Stead' hybrids and 'Ilam' azaleas are world renowned. It was at Ilam that Roland met Douglas Cook. This meeting generated an interest in Pukeiti, and Roland agreed to become one of the last Foundation Members.

After Ilam was sold to the University of Canterbury, the authorities kept the garden functioning, thus honouring the clause Roland had put in the sale of the property 'that the existing garden be maintained'. At a later date, Roland took up farming at Amberley. He still lives there today, along with some of his rhododendrons.

Roland Fraser Stead

Thomas H.N. White

Born at Awahuri, Manawatu, in 1912. Died in 1992.

Shortly after Tom White was born, his family moved to Hawke's Bay to live on a farm his grandfather had bought during the 1880s. Tom subsequently inherited a love of trees from his father. In 1944, during World War II, after his ship was sunk, Tom spent his two weeks' survivor's leave in the Cumberland woods. While there he dreamt of possessing a woodland of his own one day.

During the 1950s, when the family farm was divided up, Tom took over Barnsdale and planted the English woodland garden that he had earlier dreamt of. After his marriage to Prue (in his opinion 'one of the great amateur gardeners'), he built a homestead on it. Tom also established a Romney sheep stud amongst other farm activities. He gave time to his local community, being a JP, a vestryman for the Anglican church for some years, and a long-serving member of the local school committee.

Tom became an early member of the NZRA. (He was its Patron at the time of his death.) His interest in rhododendrons led him to become a Foundation Member of Pukeiti. He served on the Board for most of his involvement and was Chairman for a number of years. Tom was made Patron in 1987, something of which he was very proud. His son, John White, is currently serving on Pukeiti's new Board, thus maintaining a solid family tradition.

Today, Barnsdale is well known internationally among tree lovers. The trees Tom planted are now underplanted with snowdrops, bluebells and rhododendrons, including many of his own crossings.

Thomas H.N. White

Griffith William Arthur Williams

Griffith William Arthur Williams

Born in Patea 16 January 1885. Died in Hawera 12 December 1963.

Griff Williams, a second generation New Zealander, moved with his family to live in the Meremere district, inland from Hawera, in 1889. His parents took up an 80-hectare bush section there. Griff completed his secondary education at the (then) Wanganui District High School and then returned to Meremere and started work on his father's dairy farm. He was to follow that occupation until he retired.

Over the ensuing years, Griff Williams's landholdings increased to around 2000 hectares, with more than 1000 dairy cows and 9000 sheep. These farms were later divided among various members of Griff's family.

Griff took an active interest in Federated Farmers since its inception, and was a member of the first herd testing committee of South Taranaki in the early 1930s. He served as a director on the boards of three different dairy companies in the Meremere-Ohangai area over a period of 40 years and was also involved in drawing up conditions for the Sharemilkers Act, which was pioneered in Hawera. He was president of the Egmont Agricultural & Pastoral Show from 1952-61 and it was during his office term that the negotiations and purchase of Burnside, the present showgrounds, took place.

Voluntary activities included involvement with various school committees and work connected with improvements to the historic Turuturu-Mokai Reserve, scene of fighting during 1868 in the Taranaki Land Wars, also of an elaborate pa of pre-European times, considered one of the largest and best preserved in the country.

Griff was Vice-chairman of Pukeiti from 1951 to 1952. In 1953 he was elected to the position of Chairman and remained in that capacity until 1960.

Louisa Ellen Williams

Louisa Ellen Williams (née Reeve)

Born in Ashurst, near Pahiatua, 6 May 1894. Died in Hawera 6 August 1967.

Louisa ('Louie') attended primary school in Kakaramea before going on to the Patea District High School for two years. She then won a scholarship and attended the Wanganui Girls' College from 1910 until 1911. At that time her black hair was so long that she was able to sit on it. Louie went on to teach at both Normanby and Tawhiti Schools.

Louie met her future husband Griffith Williams on Mt Egmont while climbing Fantham's Peak. After their marriage at Te Teko on 14 April 1915, Griff and Louie moved into a new home called Otoki on the Allan Road, Meremere. Here they lived for 20 years and had five children.

Louie was the first president of the Meremere-Ohangai branch of the Women's Division of Federated Farmers. She held this position on three separate occasions (1943-57).

The Williamses built a lovely Tudor-style home in Ohangai in 1936. The excavation of the house site and a 2-hectare garden on several levels kept a man with a three-horse scoop busy for a year. The family moved to Bryn-y-mor (Welsh for 'the hill by the sea') in early 1937.

In 1951, Louie and Griff joined Pukeiti as Foundation Members. Both contributed financially and practically towards its establishment. For a number of years she was convenor of the Ladies Committee. Both were members of the NZRA. In the 1950s, Dr Yeates, the noted horticulturist, named a new deciduous azalea which he had propagated 'Louie Williams'.

Griff and Louie retired to Hawera in about 1960. There they developed another lovely garden in Burnside Avenue beside the A & P Showgrounds.

Opposite: An aerial view of Pukeiti with the Pouakai Ranges under cloud in the background.

CHAPTER TWO

Pukeiti — the first 25 years

The rhododendron park of Pukeiti is situated between the Pouakai and Kaitake ranges. These are on the western flank of the stand-alone 2518-metre peak of Mt Taranaki (also known as Mt Egmont) on the North Island of New Zealand.

Pukeiti, Maori for 'little hill', sits at an elevation of 520 metres and is a young lava cone of about 20,000 years old. Much of the area around Pukeiti is still covered with the Pouakai lahar ring-plain, dating back 250,000 years. This gives the extensive, rich, free-draining soil typical of the region, though now much modified by natural erosion. The hill itself has a walking track to the summit, and it had been used as a signal station during World War II. The bulk of the land area is in native bush. The elevation means that Pukeiti embraces a temperate climate, with rain being the driving force. Around 4 metres of it fall annually, making Pukeiti one of the wettest gardens on earth. Temperatures see summer highs peaking on about 26°C. The winter daytime average would be around 8–10°C. Frosts usually bottom out at -6°C. Snowfalls can occur, but they very rarely last the whole day before melting.

The prominent Taranaki surveyor, Christopher Saxton, surveyed Pukeiti free of charge. Its development was undertaken by a board drawn from throughout New Zealand, and by a local executive which undertook day-to-day management. The major layout of the gardens was developed by John Goodwin. His approach was practical.

'Back then you could see for 100 yards under the trees as goats had eaten everything out. It did have its plus side though, as it was easier to survey,' John explained. 'I covered the whole area in parallel lines, three chains apart on a compass bearing. Where the planting sites were, I just put a dot and roughly the measurement. Somebody fed back from the edge of the walk where it was more or less outlined. I'd sit here at night and work out the plans for each block. They were put down on paper and went to Pukeiti as a permanent record.'[1]

He also recalled the wet weather as being one of the worst problems encountered. A particular case in point was the Hybrid Block. After it had been bulldozed, the ground pugged rather badly and it wasn't until years later that it actually became suitable for growing plants.

Another problem was the lack of buildings. The Trust needed shelter for equipment and working parties, also accommodation for

Left: The lodge and nursery area in 1955. In the foreground are Les Boisen (left) and Jack Goodwin. Douglas Elliot

Top: Rob Hair, Curator 1960-69, mowing the lawn in front of the lodge. Pukeiti

Right: The first glasshouse (donated by Robert Ireland in 1956) and propagating frames. Pukeiti

Above: Rob Bayly standing in front of the Giant Rata in 1956. Douglas Elliott

Right: The Ackybourn Walk in the 1950s. This is the main walk through the Hybrid Block and the Maddenia section rhododendrons. Pukeiti

Development by voluntary labour, begun prior to the official opening, continued in earnest. This included fencing, scrub clearing and the opening up of old logging tracks, with variations made according to level. Planting areas along the native bush margins were also developed. All this work was overseen by Arthur Goudie, Pukeiti's first honorary curator.

The forming of a nursery area for 150 plants made feasible the Trust's early objectives. These encompassed the establishment of a collection of large-leafed rhododendrons, plus other hybrids and species for early flowering. Sympathetic with this was the preservation of the native flora and fauna.

Conditions were rugged to say the least, and there were many occasions when members thought they had got in way over their heads. The need for an adequate building became urgent, and by 1953 plans were well under way for a members' lodge. Before the lodge could become a reality, however, a roadway to the building site needed to be formed. Griff Williams brought his team of farm workers and tractors up from near Hawera in a voluntary effort towards this. Griff's son Reeve also put in a lot of time and effort at Pukeiti.

Des Corbett, an early volunteer, recalled one particular day when the road was being metalled. He sometimes worked in with farmer Arthur Richardson who, like Griff, often brought up some of his farm workers. 'The day was really wet and miserable. They were backing this truck down and it got stuck. It was about to dump river metal. One of Arthur's men said, "I think this might be the biggest waste of bloody money in the country!" At the time I had to agree with him.'[2]

Architect Raymond Syme, an early member of the Executive, designed the lodge. Several mountain rimu, given to the Trust by Bill Turchi from his adjoining property, were to be used for its construction. Russell Matthews, being publicity minded, had a former world champion axeman, Ned Shewry, there to help fell one of the trees. A qualified builder supervised the volunteer working parties who then built the lodge.

All up, the lodge was erected at a cost of £4,189. On 16 October 1954, it was officially opened by the Hon. E.B. Corbett, Minister of Lands (and Des Corbett's father). The sun shone brilliantly, in sharp contrast to when Pukeiti had been first opened three years previously. Also, 40 visitors had now become 500. The Trust Board's chairman, Griff Williams, mentioned in his speech that 'an anonymous donation of 163 acres [66 hectares] had brought the property to over 300 acres [121.5 hectares].'

a curator-caretaker. However, above the rain and lack of shelter, pests were Pukeiti's number-one problem. Aside from goats, which took six years to bring under control, possums and rabbits were also in plague proportions. A shooting and trapping programme was undertaken, and gradually pest numbers were reduced. (Over the years it is estimated that about 100,000 goats have been destroyed in the nearby Egmont National Park, which may give some idea of the magnitude of Pukeiti's problem.)

Two days after the opening, future plans for the rhododendron park were stated to include its division into blocks for exotic plants, also native trees and shrubs. (The paperwork for this had already been done by John Goodwin.)

The physical gut-busting hardships endured by all in Pukeiti's early days were tempered by a 'bush' camaraderie, topped up with gallons of tea. All shared in the understanding that each task completed was a further step towards the realisation of a collective dream. Members and volunteers came from all walks of life, some being wealthy while others were as poor as churchmice. However, rich and poor alike were on an equal footing at Pukeiti. Each donated what they could, whether it be money, time, labour, or a combination of all three.

By now membership had increased to 300, and Pukeiti was becoming more widely known overseas. It had also become a scenic reserve.

Les Boisen was the Trust's second curator (after Arthur Goudie), and its first resident curator. Upon his arrival, he found Pukeiti in a state of chaos, with him and his son having to move from room to room in the lodge, following the builders.

In his first few weeks, he helped the stonemason Doug Leighton. Between times, his job was to enrol as many new members as possible. In this he was kept up to scratch by the inimitable Russell Matthews — that human dynamo who was the spirit of Pukeiti.

Those were the days of candles, hurricane lamps, a wood range and the luxury of a phone. A special effort from the post office assisted in the connection of this. On weekends, volunteer workers

Top left: This picture from the 1950s shows Betty Elliott standing next to one of the large-leaved rhododendrons in Pukeiti's collection, a young R. sinogrande. Douglas Elliott

Top right: A view of New Plymouth taken in the 1960s from the top of Pukeiti Hill. Douglas Elliott

Below: A line of tree ferns growing down an old logging track. Pukeiti

Right: Ned Shewry contributed a lot to the development of Pukeiti, not least his experience as a world champion axeman, in 1915 and 1920, which came in handy when Pukeiti's gardens and tracks were being cleared of logs. Pukeiti

Below: Sid Snowden clearing logs the hard way, using gelignite and crow bars. Douglas Elliott

arrived in their numbers. Les Boisen ensured that the stove was kept burning to provide hot water for morning and afternoon teas. During this hectic period, Les managed to spend an hour or so in the forest, where he discovered what is now known as the Giant Rata.

From Reuthes Nursery in England arrived £500 worth of rhododendrons but there was nowhere prepared to receive the plants. About half were temporarily settled in what is now the lawn, with the remainder being looked after by Bill Turchi, a local farmer and volunteer. 'There was also this lilium seed,' Les said. 'Bulldozers had cleared the area that was to become the Hybrid Block. In desperation I sowed it as one would scatter grass seed, where the cleared land met the bush.'[3] That seed was *Cardiocrinum giganteum*, the giant Himalayan lily. Les spent two years at Pukeiti, tending to all the early plant importations, cutting new tracks and laying out the first Hybrid Block plantings.

In 1956, Robert Ireland and his wife donated Pukeiti's first glasshouse. This enabled plant material sent by overseas member supporters to be acclimatised under protected growing conditions. It was the first glasshouse to come to New Zealand after the war. Also in 1956, Rob Bayly replaced Les Boisen as curator. He had worked in Purdies Begonia Gardens and could turn his hand to almost anything. He was a brilliant fellow, according to Des Corbett. 'The hours he worked were quite ridiculous. He'd be working until ten at night and be up at the crack of dawn. Rob certainly wasn't going to get rich on what he was paid. His labour was one of love, not money driven.'[4]

The production of power to pump water and generate electricity for the lodge was something that now needed urgent attention. Rob conceived the idea of damming the Pukeiti Stream and installing a water-wheel — a smaller version of the national hydro-electric schemes. It all became a reality in 1957. An old, disused water-wheel was found at the Okato Dairy Factory, but only its bearings were salvageable. The actual plan for the 21-bucket, 3-metre water-wheel was located at the library. From this an exact replica of the original was made. Heart totara given by members from the King Country was used to construct the new wheel, a task which Rob, assisted by his uncle Jim Street (an engineer), undertook. It was then built in New Plymouth because of its weight (1.75 tonnes). When finished, the wheel was transported up to Pukeiti in sections and erected on site.

'I took my annual holidays to build the water-wheel. It almost led to divorce proceedings, but Claire and I are still together!' Rob said, tongue in cheek.[5] An enormous amount of volunteer labour went into its installation, and the construction of a dam and spillway.

Rob added that at the time, the water-wheel was quite a big thing as there were not many functional ones in New Zealand.

To begin with, the water-wheel drove a small generator at 2500 revs per minute, but this didn't last long before going to pieces. The second generator was larger and delivered 110 volts of electricity. It provided enough power for the lodge, glasshouse and a water-pump. Rob also used it to supply a speaker system that he had installed. This was for the working bees so that they could listen to the rugby and classical music, also to keep them up at Pukeiti on Ranfurly Shield days!

Mains power came to Pukeiti in about 1961 — the power generation of the old wheel only lasted two years. From this the water-wheel went on to provide water for buildings and irrigation — something it does to the present day.

In the same year that the water-wheel became a reality (1957), John Goodwin instigated the lawn. The idea came from a desire for spaciousness, but wresting a svelte lawn from what was originally swamp was never going to be easy.

Des Corbett well remembers the day he and others assisted Rob Bayly in the seed sowing. Field tiles, with a finger gap between them, were put in. Manuka (*Leptospermum scoparium*) was placed over the top as a kind of brush, then dirt covered everything up. Finally the seed was sown. 'The lawn looked really beautiful. We went up onto the veranda to have a few beers when it started to rain. We

Above: The Stead Block in 1959.
Rob Bayly

Right: The Pouakai Ranges photographed from the Cook Block, where Pukeiti was first opened in 1951. The denuded trunks of the pine trees are a legacy of 1982's Cyclone Bernie.

said, "Hooray, here comes the rain. The grass will come up." About two hours and five inches of rain later, we could see the brush at the bottom of the lawn. We had to get horse scoops and a tractor and scoop the dirt back. If you look at the lawn today, you can see a dip in it at the bottom. It was originally virtually straight.'[6]

After the drama of that day, another attempt to sow the lawn was made, but it too ended up like the first. In the end it was finally sown with a Farmall Cub tractor with a set of discs and a centre-mounted blade to level it. The lawn was raked and raked and put in like a farm paddock.

John Goodwin confided that once laid, there was a struggle to keep the lawn, as people kept wanting to put beds of azaleas in this 'nice open space'. He added that even though it was a battle at the time, it is fully justified now.[7] The lawn has served well over the years, especially on Members' Days when huge rallies would be organised. These were held in autumn and spring. The annual general meetings were (and still are) convened during the spring.

A library had been formed for members, and this included a wealth of books written by plant collectors and others. Publicity increased. Visiting journalists from New Zealand and overseas wrote articles which in turn were read by thousands. Douglas Elliott, a noted photographer, and public relations officer for the Trust, also wrote numerous articles.

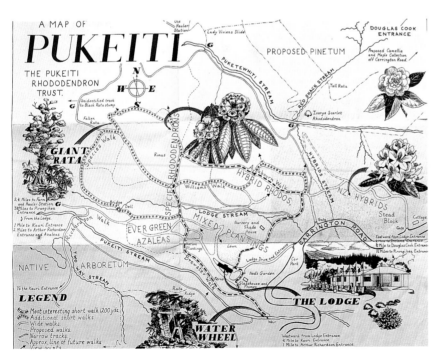

Above: During the 1960s this map was used to show the various walks around Pukeiti. (See Appendix 2 for an update on the layout of the walks today.)

The Brewster Walk is a bush track, richly decorated with a variety of ferns, as well as other native plants, that runs alongside Pukeiti Stream.

A stone wall had been built in front of the lodge with provision for flagpoles to be fitted. This was Douglas Cook's original idea. He envisaged that all the countries in the membership would be represented by their national flags. These countries included Canada, the United States, Australia, Argentina, Malaya, Africa and Hong Kong. By November 1957, 14 flags had been presented to Pukeiti.

At this time, Lord Bledisloe provided a Union Jack to be flown at the lodge. He commented that Mr Cook was one of the Trust's most enthusiastic members. Also, that a large number of members from Great Britain resulted from his personal promotion of the park when he travelled. Some of these included the Hon. Sir David Bowes-Lyon, President of the RHS 1953-61 and brother to the Queen Mother, also her sister, Lady Elphinstone.

March 1958 saw membership rise to 1650, and in excess of 1000 rhododendrons being planted. The land area was now established at 364.5 hectares, with most of it having been donated anonymously. The lodge contained many examples of generous gifts, such as silverware, Persian rugs (donated by Douglas Cook), books for the library, pictures for wall decoration, as well as equipment for use inside and out. A visitor's book kept in the lodge held an impressive lineup of names from many parts of New Zealand, as well as from overseas.

A new curator, Rob Hair, was appointed in 1960. He was to become a pivotal figure during the subsequent decade when much development took place. Rob Hair's wife, Ina, had a wonderful personality and made everyone feel most welcome. She eventually had a rhododendron named after her.

During 1960, the Trust Board's chairman, Griff Williams, disclosed that the balance sheet had a surplus of £6,000 in hand, with everything paid for. In his report he also noted that Pukeiti had 2400 members. 'This is a unique venture, and has proved that people can be interested in something for beauty and posterity, and right away from money-making.'[8]

In 1962, a new wing, complete with dining room and kitchen block, was added to the lodge. Part of the cost of this was covered by several generous members. Others gave voluntary help, especially the ladies, who several years earlier had established the Ladies Committee. It was noted at the time that without the inspiring enthusiasm of them and their helpers, the lodge would not now have such an inviting atmosphere.

Pukeiti's layout was by now well established. The main walking tracks were reshaped and drained where necessary, then grassed

down. During the mid 1960s, a second staff house was built. (Pukeiti's relative isolation necessitated staff being housed on site.) However, by the late 1960s it became apparent that a staff of two, plus volunteers, was insufficient to serve the Trust's burgeoning growth. Plans were made to increase the workforce. To cope with this, in 1973 a third staff house was built.

Despite this increase in permanent staff, the volunteer spirit was not lost, and regular working bees were held each month. Some Trust members were also members of the RHS in Great Britain. Many people there reciprocated by becoming members of the Pukeiti Rhododendron Trust.

By 1967, Russell Matthews had ploughed a large amount of resources into the Summit Road. It was also about this time that the TV tower was put in. The original track up to the Pukeiti Hill is still there, but overgrown.

Over the years, Pukeiti has seen its share of some lighter moments. John Goodwin recalled an interesting episode when the Governor-General, Sir Bernard Fergusson and Lady Fergusson visited. He apparently asked for a two-minute silence to listen to the birds. At the end of it there was one little cheep from a tomtit. It was the only sound anyone heard! (Being around midday, the birds were not at their peak of activity.)

Another incident involved the 1956 visit of Lady Vivian Younger from Scotland. She was part of the well known Scottish brewing family, and was a cheerful woman with a broad sense of humour.

Left: Rob Hair, Curator, and Laurie Hickford (both at left) greeting Governor-General Sir Bernard Fergusson and Lady Fergusson (centre foreground) at Pukeiti in 1967. John Goodwin and Tom White are on the right. Pukeiti

Bottom left: Rob Hair (left) with Governor-General Sir Arthur Porritt and Lady Porritt on the 'Gnat'. Pukeiti

Bottom right: Planting the 'Valley of the Giants' (large-leaved rhododendrons) at Pukeiti in 1968. Pukeiti

Lady Younger and Russell Matthews were walking through Pukeiti, when suddenly she fell down a muddy old logging chute, having slipped on a gelatinous black mamaku tree-fern frond.

Russell and his companions stood in silence at the top of the chute, wondering how to haul a dead peeress back up onto the track (Lady Younger being quite a large woman). Eventually, loud raucous laughter told them she had finished up in one piece.

'Apart from a very wet backside, she was okay,' John Goodwin laughed. 'After that we called her Lady Vivian Slide.'[9] Lady Younger, who was a keen gardener, later endowed Pukeiti with £500 worth of shares in her husband's brewery, and to this day they still earn an annual income.

Graham Smith appointed

The year 1969 heralded the arrival of Pukeiti's fifth curator, Graham Smith (now titled director). He was to bring a new strength of plant knowledge to the gardens, and the importation of new rhododendron species and hybrids was vigorously pursued.

Graham's interest in growing plants took root at an early age. He grew up in a flat on the outskirts of London where his father had an allotment. Flowers and vegetables were grown, and Graham found it fun to participate, except when lifting potatoes on frosty mornings! During his teenage years, Graham looked after private gardens in his spare time. He also added to his knowledge by reading everything about plants that he could find.

As the time approached to leave school, Graham was invited to become an apprentice at Regents Park in London — an offer he jumped at. Five years later, and with a good grounding as a plantsman, he was accepted for the three-year diploma course at Kew Gardens. The course involved one day of lectures and four days of practical work a week, with time spent in six different departments, ranging from the Tropical House to the tree gang. At one stage he was assigned the New Zealand collection. This was fortuitous, as Graham was intending to come and work in New Zealand for a year or two once the course was completed.

In the Temperate House, a grand titoki grew. The tree required annual pruning to prevent it from bursting through the 20-metre high roof. Upon gathering up the prunings, Graham noticed that there were bright red fruits on some of the branches. He showed them to the foreman, who said, 'That's interesting,' and departed with them. It turned out to be the first recorded fruiting of the titoki at Kew, and the event was subsequently written up in the renowned *Curtis's Botanical Magazine*.

R. *'Unique' being admired in the Hybrid Block in the 1960s.* Douglas Elliott

After Kew, the next stop was Auckland. Almost immediately after stepping off the ship with his wife, Sue, Graham began work at the Domain gardens in Auckland, looking after the Tropical House. On his first weekend duty, he noticed a newspaper advertisement for the position of curator at Pukeiti. Out of curiosity, Graham asked a fellow worker if he knew of this exotic-sounding place. 'It's wonderful,' was the reply.

Out of cheek, he sent off a letter of application, thinking it would be a great chance to see a bit of the country if he got to the interview stage. Shortly afterwards, Graham and Sue flew to New Plymouth. They were met by a Board member and driven straight up to Pukeiti. Graham recalled that they fell in love with the place from the start. 'We spent the day wandering around with our mouths open, dumbfounded by our first experience of a rainforest!'[10]

Two weeks later Graham was offered the position of curator. He accepted without hesitation, despite the fact that it would commit him to staying for sometime in New Zealand when his original intention was only to stay for a year or two. The Smiths packed up their few possessions, hopped onto the Jawa motorcycle they had bought upon arrival, and headed for Pukeiti.

In the ensuing decades Graham's relationship with Pukeiti became almost symbiotic — both flourished in each other's presence. He admits that the challenges over the years have been enormous, but the reward has been to oversee a garden of rhododendrons and other special plants to the stage where it has become one of the most important collections anywhere.

When he first began work at Pukeiti, Graham Smith was very much a gardener. Today he spends about 80 per cent of his time administrating. This presents new challenges, particularly in seeing that Pukeiti keeps abreast of developments in an ever-changing world.

The Seventies Scene

Elsie and John King arrived at Pukeiti in March 1974. They moved into the Cook House, which had just been completed six months earlier.

'John had been hired as a casual labourer,' Elsie said. She remembered that back then it was just out of the 'olden days' era. 'In the main it was a precious place to just those members whose hobby it was. Unaccompanied visitors were not generally welcomed. The main reason for this though was because they were afraid of plants being damaged or stolen.'[11]

By the time Elsie and John actually lived there, a more enlightened attitude prevailed and Pukeiti was open to the public by

donation. The donation box was held at the lodge, but often as not, some people would go round the back to avoid payment. During spring, volunteers manned the gate so visitors had no option but to be honest. A lack of shelter saw volunteers standing in wet-weather gear holding umbrellas — a not very comfortable scenario, given Pukeiti's prodigious rainfall.

Elsie and John stayed at Pukeiti for three years. One of her treasured memories is that of 30 wekas released on the mountain in an effort to re-establish them. They reared about 11 families in 22 months and one pair became very tame. Sadly, however, in no time at all the wekas had gone. Elsie believes that they succumbed to feral cats. (In January 1996, a young weka turned up at the Cook Block house and took some food, so perhaps all is not quite lost.)

After their three years up at Pukeiti, Elsie and John moved to New Plymouth, having purchased a house there. Fifteen months later (1978), Lynn Bublitz approached them to return as caretakers for the lodge, as the Trust was having a struggle to recruit anyone. The arrangement was for Elsie to be employed as the lodge caretaker, and John would be paid an hourly rate for whatever work he did. One of Elsie's tasks was to clean the rooms. She also made the workers morning and afternoon teas in the kitchen on the other side of the lodge.

Other jobs included the packing of newsletters and Christmas cards. A Mrs Mary Williams from Hawke's Bay offered plans for the Christmas cards as a fundraising effort, as by this time Pukeiti was into the business of selling itself more. The site of the present library was where people would come to the lodge for information and to buy souvenirs. By this stage Pukeiti was receiving about 20,000 visitors annually.

Elsie is well qualified to give an insight on the Ladies Committee and its establishment, for she served on it for some time and was convenor for many years. 'When Pukeiti first started in 1951, the wives would go up with their husbands and help around the gardens. After they built the lodge, the present lounge was originally a large bedroom. Back then, everyone used to sit on apple boxes with their lunches. As things improved, they decided to furnish it properly, and this was how the Ladies Committee came about. The ladies of that day of course had impeccable taste and everything had to be of the best.'[12]

There were about a dozen on the Ladies Committee at any one time, and it was not very formal. They also had a roster system in place that went well for years. Two ladies would go up every Sunday, even in winter, to hostess in case anyone visited Pukeiti. This arrangement continued right through until the Gatehouse was opened in 1987.

In the seventies the other work continued in much the same way as it had done in the past. The old Farmall tractor, or the 'Gutless Wonder' as it was called, was used for the rough work and maintenance. John King cut the outer tracks with a Gravely walk-behind mower, rather than the ride-on mowers used today.

Elsie King, now widowed, still maintains an active interest in Pukeiti's affairs. She has contributed much in the way of historical material to Pukeiti's archives, without which it would be all the poorer.

The 25th Jubilee

On Friday, 29 October 1976, Pukeiti celebrated its 25th Jubilee. This featured a rhododendron show, visits to selected gardens, and culminated in a Jubilee Dinner. Entertainment was provided by opera singer Malvina Major, and the Jubilee Speaker was Russell Matthews, Patron.

The occasion was also marked by the completion of the Display House (Pukeiti's second glasshouse). The famous English author and gardener, Frances Perry, was guest of honour at the celebrations. The glasshouse was funded by the Stanley Smith Horticultural Trust. This same organisation was also involved in the botanical exploration of Papua New Guinea, with Pukeiti once again being a beneficiary. The Display House was designed to grow and feature the subtropical Vireya rhododendrons. Today, Pukeiti is home to one of the largest collection of Vireya species in the world.

Another important addition was the construction of a new sales and administration building. It was made by apprentices from the Taranaki Polytechnic in New Plymouth, then transported up to Pukeiti by road. Shell BP and Todd Oil Services Ltd donated all of the materials. 'We admire people who try to make things like Pukeiti a going concern on their own,' Shell Managing Director Mr D. Tudhope said. 'We thought it was time they got some help.'[13]

The building was to be used as a base for the sale of the Trust's merchandise. (At one time sales had been made from under a sun umbrella!) It would also serve as an office for Graham Smith.

Above: Cyathea medullaris, *the black mamaku.*

Opposite: Looking down from Pukeiti Hill toward New Plymouth, with Paritutu, the Sugar Loaves and the chimney of the New Plymouth power station. Although close to the sea and New Plymouth, Pukeiti's elevation at over 500 metres means that it receives a lot more rain, around 4 metres annually.

CHAPTER THREE

Some early benefactors

As can be seen, Pukeiti was built on the backs of its many volunteers, with each having an individual story to tell. This chapter is devoted to just a few of those special people.

Arthur Richardson

Arthur contributed to Pukeiti in many ways, as evidenced in the previous chapter. From its inception, Arthur could be seen up at Pukeiti on almost every fine day over the ensuing ten years. On many occasions he'd be on site at seven in the morning.

Des Corbett, who was Arthur's neighbour at Okato, expanded on the man himself and what made him tick.[1] 'He'd be there with his axe, grubber and stumping jack. I remember old Arthur had a walking stick as he had a bad leg. Despite that, he'd work there all day, and when I say work, I mean hard yakka. We'd boil the billy and have our sandwiches for maybe 20 minutes for lunch, and sit down for a five-minute talk.'

'Everything was blimmin' for Arthur, as he didn't like swearing. He'd say, "On with the blimmin' work. We've got to get the blimmin' work done."'

On one occasion Des recalled he, Arthur, Ned Shewry and someone else looked into the bush and saw an area of fallen logs. It was a real mess. They said, 'That'd be a good place for a nursery.' Des went up two weeks later and the whole place had been cleaned out and dug up. 'It wasn't just a matter of cutting all that timber and hiding it in the bush. They'd taken a lot of gelignite up and blown the roots. It went virtually from second-growth bush to a garden, as it is now. Someone had to go in and clean those little areas out, and that's what they did.'

Arthur and others of his generation were people who weren't shy of doing a hard day's work. 'They'd arrive up there in their carloads from New Plymouth. All retired chaps,' Des recalled. 'Then you could have some guy who'd know all of the Latin names and just lean on a shovel, or "breastfeed the shovel" as the boys used to say!'

Above: Arthur Richardson standing next to R. 'Cornubia' in the mid 1950s. Rob Bayly

Right: Arthur Richardson (left), Russell Matthews and Stan Anchor outside the lodge in 1955. Douglas Elliott

Opposite: Two visitors dwarfed by the lush vegetation of Pukeiti, the largest public rhododendron garden in the world in a rainforest setting.

On one occasion, Arthur confided to Des, 'If I were to retire to town, it'd cost me £4,000 for a house and I'd die. I would rather spend it up here.'

Arthur Richardson also made another huge contribution to Pukeiti. He quietly purchased several blocks of land (other than Douglas Cook's original 62 hectares), and donated them anonymously to Pukeiti, together with an endowment to keep the outer tracks open. It was his acquisitions that brought Pukeiti's total land-holding up to 364.5 hectares.

Des recalled one particular story when Arthur approached his father, the Hon. E.B. Corbett, Minister of Lands (who had opened the lodge), to purchase a block of land from him. 'My father had shut up the top side of the road on the Pouakai Ranges side. He bought private land there and put it back into the reserve.'

Mr E.B. Corbett said to Arthur Richardson in his Wellington office, 'I hope I don't embarrass you with the price.'

Arthur replied, 'I paid £23 for an acre of this and £19 an acre for another block. Any price you say, Mr Corbett, will be a fair one.'

'The price is one shilling,' was the reply. This meant that the Crown didn't have to fence it off and Pukeiti's aims were identical to the Crown — to preserve the flora and fauna. That was in about 1954. This gave Pukeiti the whole 8-kilometre road frontage there now, to the corner of Pitone and Carrington Roads. One plan was to have the whole 8-kilometre stretch planted out in rhododendrons. However, it was thought that people would not then bother to come into Pukeiti itself, so they flagged that idea away.

On another occasion Des Corbett remembered Russell Matthews saying what he had given to Pukeiti. 'Old Arthur was there leaning on his axe. He just said quietly, "I haven't added up my contribution yet," and walked away.' Des then observed that some benefactors like Arthur preferred to remain anonymous, while others again enjoyed being in the limelight. 'I guess even when we get older, we're still a little bit like children!'

Arthur Richardson had the reputation of being a very hard man — a hard boss. If you didn't know him, you'd have thought of him as being rather thrifty, and very honest. You wouldn't have thought of him as being generous. In reality, Arthur was a shy, retiring, upstanding gentleman — a man who had great foresight and was successful in his own field.

'He wasn't an educated man by any means,' Des said, 'but I'd call him a great man because of his great humility.'

John Edward (Ned) Shewry

Ned was a giant of a man, and in his youth was the world's champion axeman, winning the event twice, in 1915 and 1920. He was also awarded a military medal for his services during World War I. He spent his life chopping down native bush, then did an about-turn and became an ardent conservationist. Ned developed a love of Pukeiti, in part through his association with Russell Matthews, Fred Parker and others.

Des Corbett remembered Ned as being a great old guy.[2] 'He could take the hair off his arm with his axe, it was so sharp. He would have been in his seventies then, while I was in my thirties.'

On one occasion Ned was up at Pukeiti chopping out a track called the Riverside Track. Des was with him. 'I was young and fit and didn't have a mean axe either. I was slogging into this timber, only small stuff about 6 to 8 inches through. Old Ned was coming along with his axe. I was having four or five swipes and he was going 'ping, ping', as though he was hitting it with a walking stick! His axe was that sharp. Ned was a proper bushman and knew how to cut properly.'

Ned was very much a tree man, a strong character who didn't normally like what he termed 'pansified plants'. He made one exception to this, though, with his own little garden sited in the present Covered Walk. This was always called 'Ned's Garden'. He grew polyanthus and all sorts of other things, including a red camellia at the far end. This is probably the last plant of substance which still links Ned to Pukeiti. Today a plaque marks Ned's Garden.

Ned Shewry never married. He died in 1962, and the later sale of his land at Bell Block went into the Pukeiti Trust Fund.

Stanley Smith

Stanley Smith was an Australian who worked for a time with Pukeiti board chairman Stuart Peterson. After World War II, he laid the foundations of his future wealth by the purchase and resale of American surplus war assets in the Pacific. Later investments included silver mines and many other large enterprises in Malaya and elsewhere. Although he had headquarters in several parts of the world, including London and Singapore, his more permanent home was the Bahamas.

Growing orchids was Stanley Smith's chief form of relaxation. His extensive collection was reputed to be one of the greatest in the world. According to Russell Matthews, they were literally dripping off the trees, and all were carefully tended by five gardeners.

By the time Stanley Smith became aware of the existence of the Pukeiti Rhododendron Trust, he had become a very wealthy man. It was through his warm links with Stuart Peterson that he discovered Pukeiti, and how it was launched and maintained largely by voluntary labour. Used to a hard-nosed business environment, this had a profound effect on him and he is quoted as saying, 'In this rat-race age, here were so many people willingly giving time and hard work for no pay.'[3]

Over the ensuing years, this unique aspect of Pukeiti inspired him to become one of the Trust's most enduring benefactors. Perhaps his most telling legacy was given during the 1960s. It was a book of Joseph Dalton Hooker's 1849 work *The Rhododendrons of Sikkim, Himalaya*. Of all the numerous volumes in Pukeiti's library, none enriched the collection more than this one. It is a rarity among books as it has hand-painted plates. (Only three or four copies are

Top: Stanley Smith. The Royal Botanic Gardens, Kew

Above: R. barbatum, *a magnificent hand-painted colour plate from Joseph Dalton Hooker's 1849 work* The Rhododendrons of Sikkim, Himalaya. *This rare book was donated to Pukeiti by the late Stanley Smith.*

Right: Hostas, primulas and Glenn Dale azaleas flourish beside the pond on Matthews Walk.

believed to exist today: Kew Gardens has one and Des Corbett believes Queen Elizabeth II has another.) These plates were created from drawings and descriptions made on the spot by Joseph Hooker. His botanical mission to Sikkim brought the discovery of rhododendrons previously unknown to cultivation. It was as a result of Hooker's discoveries in 1847, that many of the rhododendrons we know today were introduced.

Perhaps not so well known is that Stanley Smith had a fellow Australian millionaire friend who lived in Ireland. It seems this friend was determined never to be outdone by Stanley. Every time a large cheque arrived from the Bahamas, Pukeiti knew it was a signal to be ready for another of exactly the same amount from Ireland.

In 1967, under the chairmanship of Stuart Peterson, the Pukeiti Trust Fund was established to ensure the long-term viability of the gardens for future generations. Stanley Smith was the catalyst who got this off the ground. He wrote, 'To mark my respect and affection for my old friends Stuart and Carrie Peterson, I enclose a cheque for £10,000 to establish a Trust Fund for Pukeiti.'[4] This fund was originally administered in Wellington but is now based in New Plymouth. Today it contributes significantly to the running of Pukeiti.

Remarkably, most of Stanley Smith's generosity was exercised without his ever seeing the garden. This changed on 28 July 1967 when he and his Chinese wife, May, arrived by ship in Wellington. They flew up to New Plymouth and paid their one and only visit. (Some time after this Stanley Smith accepted patronship of the Trust.)

Curator Rob Hair felt privileged to show them around. 'It was a beautiful day and a very happy occasion. They both expressed a keen delight in Pukeiti; she in particular with the fantails and bellbirds.'[5]

In 1968, under the influence of Sir George Taylor, then Director of the Royal Botanic Gardens, Kew, Stanley Smith discussed the possibilities of setting up a Trust to support horticulture throughout the world. Unfortunately he died suddenly in the summer of 1968 before this could be done. Two trusts were subsequently set up in 1970, the benefactors being his wife, Mrs May Smith, and his daughter.

This memorable man may not have slogged away at the hard end of an axe, but his contributions by way of money and a priceless book, more than compensated. He could not donate his time or labour, but he could offer his wealth, and that is exactly what he did.

The Matthews Family

Russell Matthews (later Sir Russell), played a crucial role in Pukeiti's early development. Having said that, it would be unfair not to mention Russell's family, who were caught up in the slipstream of his boundless energy, enthusiasm and drive. His gracious wife Mary acted as the perfect foil to his powerful personality. They had four children: Elizabeth, Jill, John and Richard.

Russell was born in New Plymouth in 1896. The son of a bank manager, he received his education at the New Plymouth Boys' High School. He spent four years as an engineering assistant in the New Plymouth Borough Council and in 1914 was responsible for applying the first bitumen to a road surface in New Zealand. That was in Currie Street, New Plymouth.

Russell completed six months' military service overseas during World War I. After this he stayed on to complete a four-year engineering course at a London technical college. He returned to Auckland in 1922 and joined an engineering firm as a partner and managing director. In 1936, Russell formed Matthews & Kirkby Ltd, road-sealing contractors located in New Plymouth. From 1942 he had a road-sealing business as sole proprietor, Russell Matthews & Co. At this time his company was New Zealand's largest in this field, working throughout the country.

Above: Sir Russell and Lady Matthews at a friend's wedding during the 1980s. Lady Matthews

Right: Tupare, the garden in New Plymouth created by Russell Matthews and today owned by the Queen Elizabeth II National Trust. The magnificent Tudor replica house was designed by Mr Chapman-Taylor, a renowned architect of the time.

During the 1950s Russell sold his contracting business but retained a small bitumen supply and this became Russell Matthews Industries Ltd in 1961. The bulk bitumen installation at Port Taranaki was built during 1964-5. In 1965, Technic Industries Ltd was formed, and from 1969 undertook the manufacturing of specialised bitumen products.

Today, the Technic Group is headed by John Matthews and has been since its inception.

In 1932, Russell Matthews married Mary Elizabeth Brodie. It was also during this year that he purchased a 2-hectare block of blackberry-and-gorse-covered hillside bordering the Waiwhakaiho River. When Russell had been in Great Britain, he had become impressed with the beautiful gardens there. From this experience he harboured visions of creating an English-styled garden out of his newly purchased wilderness. The garden was named Tupare, Maori for 'garland of flowers', after the Maori tribe that once inhabited the valley. In July 1932, the first tree, a kauri, was planted. This was followed by a tulip tree and a liquidambar. Russell was a lover of trees, especially maples, and flowers.

The garden was created in three main stages; first the Elizabeth Garden was completed, then the dell, followed by the superb brick-work and walls. The waterfall, which is one of Tupare's main focal points, was constructed from stone brought in from farmland near Te Kuiti. It took four years to complete.

The magnificent three-storey Tudor replica house took 12 years to build. Designed by Chapman-Taylor, it featured adzed Australian hardwood beams, linenfold panels and a cedar shingle roof. Shingle for its reinforced concrete walls was obtained from the nearby river. Today Tupare is owned by the Queen Elizabeth II National Trust, which will ensure protection in perpetuity. Tupare was and still is a garden masterpiece.

Russell became a Fellow of the RNZIH, as well as the British RHS. His interest in rhododendrons blossomed via his association with Arthur Goudie, the noted nurseryman. 'We thought there was only one rhododendron in the world and that was the mauve one which grew wild in England,' Lady Matthews said.[6] Russell subsequently joined the NZRA. By 1951, with Tupare established, the seed of another highly focussed project germinated — Pukeiti.

Russell contributed to Pukeiti's early success in two main ways. One was in gaining new members by whatever means he could get away with, and the other was in the organisation of working bees. John Matthews remembers only too well. He spent a lot of time at Pukeiti. 'Weeks and weeks of weekends. Father had immense energy

to get together working bees. He'd spend Friday evening on the telephone, cajoling people into being there on a Saturday at the appointed time. He'd do the same thing for Sunday as well. We'd all ride up there *en masse*, be organised into working bees, then get cracking, doing whatever the project was at the time — making paths, planting areas and so on. At the end of the weekend he would simply say, "We'll see you next weekend." There wasn't an option about that.'[7]

At that time the Matthews family had a 1940s Vauxhall J. car, 'Old Gertie' as it was affectionately known. 'It used to grind its way up Carrington Road. That was a hell of a road back then. Unsealed, with all those tight curves and corners,' John said.

'When the old Vauxhall finally collapsed, the Bentley took over,' Lady Matthews added. 'Tools and other things in the back. People would move over and have their cars slide into the ditch. There'd be lots of that. We tooted on corners to warn everyone. He'd be tooting about five miles back, and everybody would be listening up at Pukeiti.'

Russell, being a roading contractor, was involved with both the lodge drive and later the road to the summit (Pukeiti Hill). He also lobbied vigorously to get Carrington Road sealed. This had originally been constructed during the Depression years. The lodge drive came complete with an underground stream. This had to be blocked up and diverted. Tons of metal fill were used to stabilise the area. Other problems were prevalent too — people problems.

'Everything wasn't all birdsong and sunshine,' as John succinctly put it. 'There were a hell of a lot of rows because there were a lot of opinionated people. Many were successful in their own right, and all held different views.'

The weather too played its part. 'There were days when it was wet, cold and miserable,' John said. 'but you were up there and work had to be done. Also, there were no facilities. You boiled a billy, had a cup of tea and your sandwiches, then on you went again.'

Later they started naming tracks after people. 'There was a great row about that. Why did this person get it and not someone else, and on it went,' John recalls. It wasn't all rows, however. 'There were people who continued to make expeditions up there time and again. They were part of the unsung core,' John said. Core members included Arthur Richardson, Howard Okey, Stan Anchor, from Anchor & Ellis the plumbers, Fred Parker of Parker's Gardens and Ned Shewry. 'These and others put in an amazing amount of time working up there. They were marvellous people and I really admired them.'

'Ned Shewry in particular later left Pukeiti a bequest,' Lady Matthews said. 'All his land at Bell Block. It was touch and go though. If it hadn't have been for Russell getting the codicil to the will signed the day before he died, that wouldn't have happened. Ned always said he was going to leave his land to Pukeiti, but never got round to it. Russell organised that for him.'

Mary too was involved in her own way. As well as family commitments, entertaining at Tupare and being on the Ladies Committee at Pukeiti, she devoted time to Sunday School and the Girl Guides. During the Depression, Mary served in a soup kitchen.

Elizabeth and Jill Matthews became involved doing a school project on weeds of New Zealand. This was to include some of the weeds at Pukeiti. 'Nobody was allowed to touch anything at Pukeiti,' Lady Matthews smiled. 'Everything was sacred according to Russell. I can almost see her exercise book now with the blank pages on Pukeiti's weeds. Poor Elizabeth!'

Tupare also played a major role in the furthering of Pukeiti's cause, both in the raising of funds and in recruitment of members. Open days were held and, more often than not, Pukeiti would be the main beneficiary. Other charities did benefit, however, and they included the Crippled Children, IHC, Salvation Army and St John's. Three thousand visitors over a weekend was not unheard of. It was the recruitment of members, however, that Russell had got down to a fine art. Numerous guests and visitors would frequently be entertained at Tupare. Douglas Cook was one.

'I can see him now,' Lady Matthews said, 'with a cane and a white safari coat, sort of a linen tropical suit and a large panama hat. He was slightly eccentric.' Other visitors included Lord Huntly and the Marchioness of Huntly, Sir Bernard and Lady Fergusson and Major General Lockhart.

Opposte: The New Plymouth City Brass Band playing during the Taranaki Rhododendron Festival. The first festival was held in 1988 and Pukeiti was naturally the festival showpiece.

Those days saw Lady Matthews ever being the charming hostess. 'Russell was a great salesman. They'd have a three-hour trip around Tupare. The grand tour — softening them up. It was always far too long and they'd come in after dark if it was winter. He'd be regaling them with funny stories and anecdotes. He was a great entertainer. That's also why people didn't want to go. They had fun. The whisky would come out, as well as rum and cloves [a cordial drink]. Also nibbles. The children would be hovering in the background.'

'Mother's poor roast would be dehydrating in the oven!' Richard laughed.

'Yes,' Lady Matthews agreed. 'He kept it simmering for about three hours before we sat down at 9 o'clock for dinner. In those days you normally ate at six. I used to have to get the book out at the right psychological moment. "Mary, get the membership book, will you?" They'd sign up before they knew where they were!'

From ordinary worker to the Governor-General — no one escaped signing up for Pukeiti, save those who were already members. 'People were never aware of being coerced into signing,' Lady Matthews added. 'He was so charismatic, and the affection in his boundless enthusiasm rubbed off onto everybody.'

She then commented on his other side. 'Russell was actually very autocratic and dictatorial — disliked anyone disagreeing with him. He fell out with everyone in turn. One week they'd be a great mate, and the next they'd be a silly old such and such. There was a lot of that. He was very naughty. Yet because of that, in a funny sort of way, his enormous energy probably pushed people and things along...'

Another method Russell employed to drum up membership was in the use of film shows. He had been to the Coronation in England in 1953, and took lots of newsreels of it. There were also films of other places. John remembered them well. 'There were tours around New Zealand to horticultural meetings. They were quite remarkable and were organised on the basis of a film evening. You'd go in a circuit: Wanganui, Marton, Palmerston North. Or down to the South Island, the same sort of thing.'

Lady Matthews added some of her memories. 'Some of the halls were so small that the projector — which was a huge thing on a pedestal — had to go outside in the paddock, beaming through the door and onto the screen to get a big enough image.'

'There'd always be a drama about it,' John continued. 'Finding a socket. Then often a bulb would burn out. Sometimes we had a spare, sometimes we didn't. It did fluster Father, but he always rose above it. He'd show this film, whatever it was, then give a speech on Pukeiti. All that was pretty standard stuff. At the end of it, he'd

stand at the doorway or sit behind a table next to the doorway. "I'm not letting anybody out. Nobody is to leave this hall without joining up for Pukeiti. I've come all this way. Everybody's doing a great job and we need your membership, so if you don't mind please, I'll sign you up on the way out." And he'd do just that. That's another way he raised the membership by hundreds and hundreds of people.'

Russell also had a tremendous input into the lodge. The gates were copied from Tupare, and the black and white timbering of the lodge is also reminiscent of Tupare, as is the fireplace. The stones for this were obtained from the Waiwhakaiho River by Lady Matthews. 'There was a row about the beams where you stand outside on the veranda. I don't know who "they" were. "They" didn't want the fireplace — those designs — but they got them of course,' she said.

Fred Parker did the brickwork around the lodge. On one occasion, taking a truckload of bricks up to Pukeiti turned into a Laurel and Hardy affair. 'Father thought he'd borrow one of his [the firm's] lorries. It was a Thames Trader and had an Eaton differential — a form of overdrive which my father wasn't used to. This thing was in overdrive so it had very little power. It got slower and slower. They changed gears but it made no difference. They stopped and unloaded some bricks, went on a bit more, stopped again and unloaded yet more bricks. My father was cursing this useless truck! They even tried to go in reverse. In the end they got Stan Riddick, who was the foreman, to bring out another truck. Poor Stan. He knew exactly what was wrong!'

Among some of the gifts given to Pukeiti was a teapot. 'Mrs Turchi gave Russell a huge enamel teapot with a couple of tea towels inside,' Lady Matthews said. 'And it's not as if they were well off. They lived just down the road from Pukeiti in a tiny shed with corrugated-iron walls. It was surrounded by tree stumps and looked like the 1860s. They were both involved. She'd make the tea while Bill would be digging and working with people like Ned Shewry.'

Then there was a mirror. 'We shouldn't mention that really, as it's not kind,' Lady Matthews added. 'A mirror, which was scalloped around the edges, was given to Russell. We all looked at it and thought, it isn't Pukeiti. The unfortunate thing was relegated to the women's rest room.'

Russell was thought of as principally being an organiser. He liked nothing better than to be in his old clothes and boots directing people. 'This was probably a hand down from being in business,' John said. 'If you broke Pukeiti up into little projects, he'd like to get each one ticked off in turn.'

With Douglas Cook living over in Gisborne, Russell took on a bit more authority and was able to get away with things. 'He wasn't

Left: The Ayckbourn Walk leading down to the yellow rhododendron 'Saffron Queen'.

Below: Looking down to the Founders' Garden, dedicated in 1996, just outside the Gatehouse.

Left: Pukeiti in mid winter with the snow-capped Pouakai Ranges in the background.

Right: This path, leading across to the Matthews Walk, features the white azalea 'Snow Storm' on the left, with the pink R. arboreum on the right.

popular with a lot of people,' Lady Matthews said. 'This was quite sad really, because he was the heart and soul of Pukeiti.'

Often Russell would come home to Tupare and say he was going to resign. It could have been prompted by a meeting at Pukeiti, or a working bee where there was something he had disagreed with. 'He got very distressed on many occasions about contrary points of views. We took his threats to resign rather pragmatically,' John said. 'He found it difficult to resign of course, because that would have meant handing it all over to somebody else. Also, what was all the dedication about if he pulled out?'

From the 1960s, there emerged a levelling-off period. The loyalty returned, but Russell's passion had diminished as there was no need for the huge amount of energy and work, apart from the creation of the Pukeiti Summit Road in which he was involved.

Russell's passion was rekindled early in 1967 when he brought Mr Charles Puddle, the head gardener of the world-famous gardens at Bodnant, North Wales, over to New Zealand. Mr Puddle came with an impressive list of credentials. He had been awarded the A.J. Waley Medal for work with rhododendrons, and also been made an Associate of Honour of the RHS for distinguished services to horticulture in the course of his employment. In 1962 he received the Victoria Medal of Honour, the Society's highest award, and three years later he was made a Member of the Order of the British Empire in Her Majesty's Birthday Honours, for services to horticulture.

Mr Puddle was set to work for the University of Canterbury, but they could not pay his full salary. They asked Pukeiti to contribute £300 a year for part of his services. Russell marvelled at the thought of having a world authority to help develop Pukeiti further. The proposal was put before the Pukeiti Board, but lack of funds was a problem. Russell was financially committed to the Summit Road, so he sought assistance from the Todd sisters. They agreed to donate £100 a year for three years to help secure Mr Puddle's services. In February 1967, the Board unanimously approved Mr Puddle's appointment (subject to his acceptance), although the Executive was 'very disturbed' about this and suggested that the Board reconsider the question.

By July it was all over as Stuart Peterson, Chairman of the Pukeiti Trust, nullified the Board's decision. 'There was a row about that as Russell had sponsored Mr Puddle's visit and, along with four others, had paid for his fare. That didn't go down at all well,' Lady Matthews said. In the aftermath of this, the Todd sisters agreed to their donated monies being redirected into the Summit Road project. By this stage Russell was ill. He had a detached retina and was also awaiting surgery for his arthritic hips. He resigned from the Board on 24 June 1967.

However, Russell's resignation and poor health did not diminish the flow of often blunt letters that he wrote. In one he bemoaned that Pukeiti 'must be run as a business, not as a Playboy's outfit', while in another he complained about sheep being brought in. The brickbats though were always tempered with bouquets, as was his way.

From the 1970s, a more democratic regime evolved, and it became more self-perpetuating. These things aside, however, Russell never lost his interest in Pukeiti, and in 1972 he was made its Patron.

Russell Matthews was awarded the OBE in 1971. This was in recognition of his work at Pukeiti, and in other fields such as horticulture, industry and philanthropy. He was made a Knight Bachelor in 1981 and was knighted in 1982.

After being ill for some time, Sir Russell Matthews died on 25 November 1987, aged 91. The Matthews family are justifiably proud of Sir Russell's achievements at Pukeiti.

CHAPTER FOUR

Developments (and some disasters) 1979–96

The year 1979 had seen the arrival of Pukeiti's third glasshouse, donated by Ewen and Sylvia Perrott. Ewen Perrott had been growing rhododendrons by the tens of thousands when he decided not to continue and instead set up his two sons in dairying. Pukeiti was the beneficiary of this decision. John King, Dave Whitehead and Graham Smith went up to Te Awamutu to help dismantle the glasshouse. John Matthews sent up one of his trucks to bring it back, free of charge.

Up to this point, Pukeiti had survived on the subscriptions and generosity of its members, plus visitor donations. The timely donation of the Perrotts' glasshouse enabled a 'plants for members' scheme to be initiated. This proved popular from the outset and is now an annual event. The new glasshouse also freed up the original propagation house, donated in 1956, for re-use as a quarantine centre.

Many esteemed people visited Pukeiti over the years. On 12 March 1980, their ranks were swelled by the Rt Hon. Robert Muldoon, Prime Minister of New Zealand, who had a keen interest in plants, especially liliums.

By 1981, membership had risen to 3500, and 10,000 rhododendrons and other plants were being grown at Pukeiti. Donations by banks and businesses were used for things such as building an information centre and upgrading glasshouses.

The Trust employed a curator, two assistants, a caretaker and a lodge custodian. It also made use of various government employment schemes. A new pond was developed where a creek had once flowed, and close by part of the old log-hauling trench was opened up to view.

The cloud formation shows off to perfection the tree ferns and rhododendrons on the Stead Walk leading up to the Stead Block.

Cyclone Bernie

Easter Friday, 9 April 1982, turned into Black Friday as Cyclone Bernie, striking from the southeast, roared through Pukeiti with a ferocity that had not been seen since 1908. Des Corbett had some visitors over from Napier. As it was blowing quite strongly, he took them up to Pukeiti, believing that it would be calm up there. 'As it happened, we were too scared to walk from the lodge to the road. This huge windstorm swept down over the ranges. You could hear it coming and the trees breaking.'[1]

More than 3000 trees were blown down and over 100 rhododendrons met with a similar fate — many being as old as the Trust itself. The pine plantation, established in 1970 under the guidance of Grant Maxwell, was totally decimated. With it had gone a future source of income. All the tracks were blocked by fallen debris. On top of this, Pukeiti was without power for 20 hours, and the phone for five days. Road access to New Plymouth was cut off for eight days. On the plus side, there were no injuries to staff or visitors, and very little damage to buildings.

The Hybrid Block, the original major planting of rhododendrons, was so extensively damaged that a new approach to landscaping had to be found. Instead of having individual plants or groups in mown grass, it was decided to have large, free-form beds. However, resources at the time only allowed this to be implemented in the Hybrid Block.

Pukeiti may have been down but it was certainly not out. Members and volunteers picked themselves up from their aftershock and got stuck in. Clearing the mammoth mess took first priority. Six hundred rimu trees were then planted throughout the reserve in an effort to fill the many gaps. Upon the arrival of spring, new growth burst forth and more rhododendrons were planted. Pukeiti's recovery was under way.

On 10 September 1983, the planting of what was believed to be New Zealand's first private commercial rimu plantation took place. Twenty volunteers planted 1000 trees in the former pine plantation, the intention being that they would eventually be used as an income-earning resource. Trust Chairman Lynn Bublitz has since intimated that as it could be 100 years before the rimus matured, future Trust members may prefer to conserve them as a reserve. Since then, additional plantings of rimu, kahikatea and totara have been added, and this is now known as the Podocarp Block.

One of the most tranquil spots at Pukeiti is surely the moss-encrusted water-wheel on Pukeiti Stream.

Also in September, the New Zealand Synthetic Fuels Corporation presented Pukeiti with a cheque for $40,000 to establish a Synfuels-sponsored apprenticeship for at least four years. In return, the Trust was to provide five years' landscaping consulting services to the Synfuels project at Motunui.

In 1984, a World Wildlife Fund campaign to save endangered species of plants was launched at the autumn meeting of the Trust. Pukeiti had been chosen as the venue because it had a very fine collection of rare and endemic native plants. Of the existing 250,000 flowering plant species in the world today, it is predicted that fewer than 40,000 will exist by the middle of the next century. 'In New Zealand there are 1800 species of native plants, 80 per cent of which are endemic. More than 200 of these are classified as rare, and ten are in danger of extinction,' Sir William Gilbert, Chairman of the New Zealand Branch of the Fund said.[2]

By now, Pukeiti was home to the Southern Hemisphere's largest collection of rhododendrons — one of the major collections in the world. Annual visitor numbers hovered at around the 20,000 mark. Despite this, Carrington Road was still not 100 per cent bitumen sealed. However, by September 1985 the 1.3 kilometres of metal just shy of the Trust's entrance was sealed. This left a 2-kilometre stretch of metal between Pukeiti and Pitone Road which had yet to be done.

The Gatehouse and Conference Centre

The Gatehouse project grew out of the realisation that, apart from the lodge, Pukeiti had no real facilities for the public. Sometimes, if it was quiet, a cup of tea could be offered to a non-member. In those early days, however, it was a little bit frowned on to have too many non-members in the lodge. For a number of years volunteers did Devonshire teas under the lodge, but ended up running themselves ragged.

Public toilets were another problem. The only facilities in the place were a 'Mens' stuck down in the basement and a 'Ladies' at the far end of the lodge. By 1984, it was decided that enough was enough. A new amenities building, to be sited next to the gate, was decided upon. For the first time in its history, the Pukeiti Rhododendron Trust appealed to the community at large for funds. Thus in August 1984, the Gatehouse Appeal for $200,000 was

launched. The total cost to build was estimated at $300,000.

Terry Boon was assigned to do the design work. The Gatehouse, when opened, would provide a reception centre, souvenir shop, restaurant facilities and an attached flat for the manager. This would then allow refurbishment of the lodge to provide overnight accommodation for Trust members. It was hoped to commence building within 18 months.

Fifty thousand dollars were donated within a short period of time, most of it from business houses in Wellington and Auckland. The Taranaki Savings Bank launched the local appeal with a cheque for $7,000. Soon to follow came a $4,000 donation by Shell Todd Oil Services Ltd. Later in the year, $7,000 was raised from the opening of Tupare.

In August 1985, the appeal benefited from the late Ned Shewry's estate. The land Ned owned had been held in limbo for 21 years at his request. He believed that if Pukeiti survived for more than 20 years, then it would continue.

By this time, $100,000 had been raised. Applications were then made to the Lotteries Board and Development Levy Fund for further funds. In November, Trust executive chairman Lynn Bublitz announced that the Gatehouse would be built in stages as finance became available. Construction began in January 1986, but was not without its problems. The building Pukeiti eventually finished up with was different from the one first envisaged.

Originally the building was going to be up against the gateway, but according to the Taranaki County Council it would have been too close to the road. It had to be sited about 6 metres south, which would then make it beyond the road reserve. 'When we did this, however, all the ground fell away,' Graham said. 'We had to prop the thing up high, so it was literally built on a basement. The storage underneath could one day be used for some display centre or conference room. That was the accident which really set it off.'[3]

This was for the future, however. By May 1986, building had stopped as funds had run out, with $150,000 spent thus far. Another $100,000 could have seen it open by spring. Cost estimates had now risen to $350,000. Money started coming in again from various sources, including $25,000 donated by some of the Trust's members, who also sponsored a lot of the furniture.

Vaccinium stapfianum var. oreifolium *from Thailand happily growing on a tree fern trunk. The metal collar on the tree behind is to deter possums from climbing the tree and eating out the crown.*

Left: The official opening of the Gatehouse on 1 November 1986. The two men with the ribbon are David Tudhope (left), Pukeiti Board Chairman, and Philip Woollaston, then Undersecretary for Conservation, Environment and Local Government. Taranaki Newspapers Limited

Below: Keshab Pradhan, President of the Sikkim Nature Conservation Council, first Secretary to the Government, Sikkim, admiring R. arboreum kermesinum *at Pukeiti in 1990.* Pukeiti

On Saturday, 1 November 1986, the Gatehouse was officially opened by Mr Philip Woollaston, Undersecretary for Conservation, Environment and Local Government. He was due to present a cheque for $35,000, a Government Tourism grant towards the Gatehouse building. This inadvertently got left behind. (It did arrive a week later.)

When finished in mid 1987, final costs for the Gatehouse complex had escalated to $460,000, but through a mix of Trust funds, donations, grants and sponsorship, the building was completed debt-free. If it had to be built today, Pukeiti would not be able to afford it.

The Gatehouse was opened to the public on 1 July 1987. At that time, however, the Pukeiti Trust did not see itself as having enough business expertise to run it. Bill and Pat Campbell were the first enthusiastic lessees. An estimated 20,000 people visited Pukeiti during 1986, and they were keen to expand on that. The Gatehouse was (and still is), open all year round, except on Christmas Day. In 1989, the lease was sold to Nick and Rose Randall, who stayed until 1993, when Beverly Grant and Jacqui Lockhart took over. Beverly and Jacqui subsequently departed in late 1995.

As the years passed, it became obvious that the Gatehouse had not turned out to be a bank manager's dream. The time had come for Pukeiti itself to take over the helm. A fresh approach and new ideas, orientated towards the gardens, were needed.

Pukeiti tends to have two different types of visitor. One is the keen gardener, who usually comes when the rhododendrons are at their peak. Tourists make up the second type. For them Pukeiti is just another experience, like 'doing' the geysers in Rotorua. Most people who visit, irrespective of their reasons, are usually on the lookout for a specific souvenir — for example, items like teaspoons with Pukeiti on them, specially designed indigenous postcards, etc. Guided evening walks, combined with a meal during the summer months is a service that is proving to be quite popular.

The Gatehouse and Conference Centre offer a breathtaking venue for weddings and conferences. Pukeiti offers a location second to none — something more wedding and conference participants are becoming aware of.

In 1987, the Pukeiti Rhododendron Trust accepted affiliation with the Trust of the Seibu Akagi Botanical Institute in Japan, the aim being to promote friendship, plus an exchange of information, plants and propagating material between New Zealand and Japanese horticulturists, to benefit the people of both countries. The formal agreement was signed on 7 November 1987. In connection with this, six varieties of rhododendrons from Taranaki were planted in the Seibu Akagi Nature Observation Park next to Mt Akagi near Tokyo.

Above: Two people flew from Japan to spend four days drying Meconopsis *flowers for a Japanese Expo. Pukeiti was the only place in the world where these blue poppies were open at just the right time.* Taranaki Newspapers Limited.

Left: Scientist Xiao Tiao-Jiang (John) of the Kunming Botanical Institute, China, on a Pukeiti-sponsored Camellia reticulata *DNA analysis programme.* Taranaki Newspapers Limited

Cyclone Bola

Cyclone Bernie was almost a fading nightmare when, on 8 March 1988, another cyclone of even greater magnitude struck Pukeiti, again from the southeast. Cyclone Bola, packing magnum-force winds of 165 km/h plus, split many 500-year-old native trees down the middle. Others were pushed over, while some lesser trees and rhododendron bushes were sent flying through the air, never to be seen again. It looked as though a giant had squashed Pukeiti underfoot, with trees strewn about in all directions like discarded matchsticks. In one disastrous night Pukeiti lost 10,000 of its trees. Fortunately the large-leafed rhododendrons, being completely sheltered, were spared from Bola's onslaught.

In the aftermath Graham Smith wept as he surveyed Bola's rampage. 'We lost a huge number of very old trees that have obviously not seen the likes of such a horrendous storm before. We have to assume it won't happen again for a very long time and work to restore Pukeiti to its former glory.'[4]

Members and volunteers, many of whom came from all over New Zealand, once again began the stoic and grim task of another mighty cleanup in preparation for replanting. Over 2000 man hours were put into clearing the garden of debris during the first month alone. Pukeiti stayed open and visitors still came, though in lesser numbers during this trying time.

The Park's sheer scale necessitated a woodland setting for many of the gardens, with the more exotic species being grown in a display house. A permanent staff of six people tended to everything. 'We cannot expect miracles on a 360-hectare property with such a small number of staff,' Graham said. 'This is where the service rendered by our volunteers is so invaluable. We only have to look at their huge effort in the wake of the two cyclones.' Membership too was commensurate with the property's size. With over 3200 members, the Trust was the largest private club in New Zealand.

Top: This view from the Gatehouse shows the bush 'Bolarised' after Cyclone Bola hit in March 1988. Lynn Bublitz

Centre top: Cyclone Bola caused enormous damage, with winds of over 165 km/h splitting many 500-year-old trees. Pukeiti

Centre: Cyclone Bola destroyed not only the bush surrounding the gardens but also the walks and beds. Lynn Bublitz

Left: The borders by the Gatehouse restored after Cyclone Bola.

Opposite: The pond area, looking back to the Pouakai Ranges.

A fallen tree fern close to where Lady Vivian Younger, on a visit
in 1956, experienced at first-hand the old logging chutes that can
be seen around Pukeiti. After this incident she was known as
Lady Vivian Slide.

The Taranaki Rhododendron Festival

October 1988 ushered in the first Taranaki Rhododendron Festival. Pukeiti, despite being bloodied by Bola, rose to the occasion and put on a superb display to be the festival showpiece.

The idea of a rhododendron festival evolved about the same time as the Gatehouse. Discussions started at one of the Trust's meetings. During the 1980s, Pukeiti was having problems coping with the Labour Weekend rush. This was seen as being a bit early for Pukeiti, whose gardens peaked after October 25. Also, the aim was to stretch out the viewing season so that people could then enjoy the experience, rather than feeling jam-packed like sardines. At the time, Dunedin was the only place in New Zealand which had anything like a rhododendron festival.

Pukeiti discussed the idea with Elaine Gill at Tourism Taranaki. A festival on such a scale would need to be a combined effort, organised out of Pukeiti. The first Steering Committee meeting of the Taranaki Rhododendron Festival was held in the Council Chambers on 1 February 1988, its purpose to gauge support for the concept of a Rhododendron Festival to be held from 29 October until 5 November. These dates had been chosen for three reasons:

1. Tony Schilling, Deputy Curator of Wakehurst Place, United Kingdom, would be a guest at Pukeiti during this time.
2. The festival would follow the Rhododendron Conference that was to be held in Palmerston North. It would therefore attract South Island visitors to Taranaki.
3. The blooms were at their best during this time, and theoretically the weather was usually more settled.

Tourism Taranaki provided $5,000 to cover the cost of a television advertising campaign, also for a colour brochure to be printed. The *New Zealand Gardener* asked to be involved and kept up to date.

The inaugural festival was extremely successful, with Pukeiti being at its heart, and foundations were laid for it to become an annual event. In 1990, around 11,000 people visited the festival. On one Sunday alone, 2000 people passed through Pukeiti's gates. This included nine coachloads of tourists. By 1991, promotions of the event had spread to the United States, Australia and Japan. In 1992, Pukeiti received the Tourism Taranaki 'Excellence in Tourism' Award for its major contribution to the Rhododendron Festival's success.

Taranaki was well and truly on the map as *the* place to go for great gardens in general, and rhododendrons in particular. The numbers of gardens opened to the public peaked at 130. Today it is restricted to around 100.

As the years passed, Pukeiti's pivotal role in the festival diminished. People visited other gardens at the expense of Pukeiti, perhaps because many of them were only open during the festival, whereas Pukeiti was seen to be accessible all year round. Trying to dispel local apathy is always difficult, and bearing this in mind 1995 saw a major change of focus for the garden during the Festival. Special events were organised as added attractions, including a flower show. There was a marquee with petanque, a couple of bands and guided walks. This new approach proved to be a great success, with Pukeiti recording more than double the visitor numbers it had the previous year.

Coinciding with the first Taranaki Rhododendron Festival, on Saturday, 29 October 1988, two special events took place at Pukeiti. One was the naming of a new cross-bred rhododendron after the Trust's late Patron, Sir Russell Matthews. The other was the re-naming of the Species Walk to honour Sir Russell and Lady Matthews. Lady Matthews officially dedicated the walk.

'Both acts fit nicely the Trust's policies of naming tracks only after Foundation Members, and naming exceptional New Zealand-raised hybrid rhododendrons after people who have made an outstanding contribution to Pukeiti,' the Trust Board's chairman, David Tudhope, said on this occasion.

Pukeiti is sometimes the base for rescue operations in the neighbouring Egmont National Park. Here a RNZAF Iriquois helicopter lands on the lawn in front of the lodge. Pukeiti

In 1993 the Covered Walk was opened. This area was designed to display Pukeiti's extensive collection of Vireya (tropical) rhododendrons. From left to right: Graham Smith, Director; David Lean, Mayor, New Plymouth District Council; David Tudhope; Willie Still and Lynn Bublitz.
Taranaki Newspapers Limited

Display House extensions

The burgeoning Vireya rhododendron collection caused a re-think on how to best display them to the public. In 1987, a proposal for a covered walk — literally a bush walk with a roof overhead — was put to the New Plymouth Rotary Club. Then with assistance from local companies, a new Display House was built in 1989 to house Pukeiti's many hundreds of Vireyas, plus other interesting tender plants. Even after this though, more changes were made.

The Display House was removed in February 1993 and replaced with an extension of the Covered Walk. This was later joined up by internal staircases to the Perrott House, which in turn had been retired from plant propagation and converted to a new Public Display House. From July through to November 1993 it was landscaped in a semi-formal manner to house a collection of rhododendrons from Borneo and Malaysia, also bromeliads and tropical foliage plants requiring warmer conditions than the other glasshouses provided. Ewen and Sylvia Perrott, the original donors of Perrott House in 1979, were on hand to re-open it on 13 November 1993.

Also in 1993, master hybridiser Felix Jury was awarded the Veitch Memorial Gold Medal by Britain's prestigious RHS. He was nominated by the Pukeiti Rhododendron Trust on the suggestion of plant-hunter Keith Adams. Felix was a great collector of plants, and his garden at Tikorangi would have one of the most eclectic collections in the country. (Felix Jury passed away in March 1997).

Financial problems in the nineties

During June 1990, Director Graham Smith visited the Waipahihi Botanical Gardens at Taupo. These had been established using Pukeiti as a model. However, by November of that year things were not looking so rosy for Pukeiti itself. Membership declined, dropping to 2500 from a high of just over 3000 a couple of years before. To top it off, a deepening financial crisis emerged. This saw the Trust having to dip into its funds to meet a budget shortfall of $30,000. One staff member also had to be shed.

Graham attributed one of the reasons to a downturn in the economy. With regards to the membership 'plunge', upon checking, it was discovered that a lot of members were unfinancial. The situation came to light when the office operations were moved up to Pukeiti from New Plymouth, and the membership set-up looked at on the computer. There were a lot of anomalies in the system.

On the plus side, visitor numbers were up. Also, a positive response to a newsletter appeal saw 70 per cent of those who replied renew their subscriptions. Another plus saw the last 2-kilometre stretch of Carrington Road between Pukeiti and Pitone Road being sealed. This was achieved in February 1991.

The year 1991 marked Pukeiti's fortieth anniversary. The gardens were now home to 10,000 rhododendrons, flowering from June through to March, with October-November being the peak blooming months. Substantial new landscaping took place. Many of the original plants had reached maturity, and others were well past their best. The cyclones, too, had left their destructive stamp on the gardens.

On 2 November 1991, Caroline and Nicholas de Rothschild toured Pukeiti as part of a 10-day visit. Mr de Rothschild chairs Exbury Enterprises — part of Exbury Gardens which his grandfather started to build in 1919 near Fawley, Southampton, on the Beaulieu River. This woodland garden, covering around 100 hectares, took 20 years to complete. By 1991, Exbury boasted 1,000,000 plants and hosted 140,000 visitors. It is the international centre of rhododendron development, and more hybrids are developed there than at any other location in the world.

Mr de Rothschild was in New Zealand to find out about species and examples of rhododendrons and azaleas being grown here. He was particularly taken with the tree fern, saying that it gave Pukeiti a wonderful architectural look. He also concurred that in the past the rhododendron had been considered a rich man's plant, but now it was a plant for all.

Top: Dr George Argent, a Vireya rhododendron specialist with the Royal Botanic Garden Edinburgh, at Pukeiti in 1990. He is about to photograph R. *'Flamenco Dancer'.* Pukeiti

Above: Shadehouse 1, 1988, full of young rhododendrons being grown on for future planting. Pukeiti

Ailsa Andreoli (7) left, head gardener
Andrew Brooker and Dana Brophy
(9) planting a rimu seedling. They
were part of a 50-strong troupe from
Rahotu School's new entrants to
standard two class that planted
seedlings at Pukeiti in July 1993.
Taranaki Newspapers Limited

October 1992 saw Pukeiti's financial plight continue, despite efforts to contain it. Another $30,000 was uplifted from Trust funds to pay off a shortfall. Visitor numbers had levelled off and membership was still static. Income from the Trust Fund dropped as well, in line with lower interest rates, but a Shell Todd Oil Services Ltd sponsorship helped to maintain cash flow.

A number of schemes were introduced to bulk up membership, and the deficit was seen in part as a continuing throwback to previous years. On the positive side, the Trust had more or less balanced its budget over the last year, and was not about to roll over and die.

In November 1992, a Lower Hutt couple, Kenneth and Iris Gittings, bequested $250,000 to Pukeiti. It was hailed as a wonderful and very timely boost. This was added to the Trust Fund, which by now contained $450,000. Pukeiti would benefit in the coming years by drawing on the interest.

Educational promotions

Pukeiti plays a small but growing part in education, especially school education. Schools such as the New Plymouth Boys' High and the Taranaki Polytechnic bring trainees to Pukeiti who are doing horticulture as part of their curriculum. The gardens are seen as an 'open classroom', and are invaluable in the compilation of school projects.

In spring 1993, a 50-strong troupe from Rahotu School's new entrants to standard two class planted about 30 rimu seedlings, this being part of their study on native trees. Schoolchildren involvement is encouraged, for they are seen as the future members and lifeblood of Pukeiti. Graham Smith intimated that he would like to see every school in Taranaki make use of Pukeiti's facilities for their pupils. He also emphasized that schools are never charged for access to the gardens. The theatre/display area is seen as having an unlimited potential for classroom work as well.

Packages of information would be provided to cater for different levels of proficiency. Education labelling is something else to be looked at. When students go round, there would be key things to look for and write about. Relationships with animals and people, birds, botany and the weather — all tied in with each other to make it a pleasant learning experience.

Some money left over from a Taranaki Savings Bank donation has been earmarked for a video projector so that videos can be projected onto a screen for viewing in the theatre area. It will also feed off a computer with CD-ROMs going through it. Equipment can eventually be added to this, making up a class situation which could be either sophisticated or simple, as required.

Overseas exchange facilities are something else that Pukeiti frequently gets asked about. Requests come in almost monthly from people all around the world wanting to come and work in the gardens — with the possibility of one of Pukeiti's staff members going over to their country. Graham Smith is somewhat amused at the prospect. 'They don't have any idea of how small Pukeiti is. They think we're a large organisation with 50 to 100 staff, herbarium, laboratories and all of that. They're amazed when we tell them otherwise.'[6] He conceded that it would be a wonderful learning experience for everyone, but practicalities limit Pukeiti to concentrating on local schools for the present.

On a different tack, Pukeiti also sees the need to do things in other languages, such as German and Japanese. Seasonal leaflets are another possibility. The visitor can then see what is in flower at a particular time of the year. One was done on the large-leafed rhododendrons, and this created a lot of interest. These, too, could be extended into other languages. In the end, however, resources, both in terms of people and money, are required for anything further than what is currently being achieved.

The year 1996 saw Pukeiti at the forefront of public rhododendron gardens with a worldwide reputation for expertise amongst growers of these popular plants. Equally prominent in such circles is Director Graham Smith, a recognised international authority on rhododendrons who is in great demand as a speaker on the overseas circuit. Despite some massive setbacks, in 45 years Pukeiti has secured for itself a place on the world stage.

CHAPTER FIVE

Pukeiti today — and tomorrow

Today sees Pukeiti standing very much at the crossroads on a number of fronts. Since Cyclone Bola, volunteer labour declined, in part because it wasn't being encouraged. Membership too was still suffering, despite earlier schemes to bolster it. Director Graham Smith recognises that the system and attitudes have to change. Aligned with this, a new constitution is being drawn up. Graham believes that members and staff need to feel they're more than dollars and cents, that they are part and parcel of what Pukeiti is.

Since instituted in 1995, the regular monthly working bee has gained in popularity. Twenty to 30 people have been coming in on a Saturday and much of the early enthusiasm has returned. Members feel as if they belong to something of value now, more so perhaps than before. The new enlightened 'people/worker' policy has cost Pukeiti money to achieve, but it has got more back in goodwill because of it. In line with this, a visitors' survey and a members' survey have been undertaken. The results so far have been encouraging. As might be expected, such surveys confirm that individual perceptions of Pukeiti are varied.

Currently, Graham Smith is working on Pukeiti's five-year plan. High on the agenda is membership, with cost seen as an inhibiting factor. Every time subscriptions rise, a five or 10 per cent loss in membership occurs. Pukeiti needs to sign up about 200 members a year to keep on an even keel. The attrition rate is about that, due to an aging membership. Approximately 60 per cent of members are over 60 and younger people are always being sought. This is not easy, however, as different age groups identify with different pastimes. Pukeiti has to compete against a broad range of activities, many of which were not available 20 years ago.

Above: The Director of the Pukeiti Rhododendron Trust, Graham Smith.

Left: The team at Pukeiti. From left to right: Noel Bullot (Taskforce Green worker), Alan Anderson (Gardener), Graham Smith, Andrew Brooker (Head Gardener), Peter Davis (Caretaker/Handyman), Karen Davis (Restaurant Co-ordinator) and Grant Carroll (Business Manager). (Since this photo was taken, Helen Topliss has been employed as Receptionist/Administration).

Opposite: An aerial view of the Gatehouse, lodge and lawn.

Graham firmly believes it is important to remember what Pukeiti is all about — and that is the garden. Because of this, the Trust has to resist the temptation of going over the top in an effort to be a crowd pleaser. Suggestions have ranged from having a gondola on top of Pukeiti Hill, to a railway starting out from the front lawn. Others think that having billboards like the 'Shell Hybrid Block', the 'McDonald's Large-Leaf Area', or even flashing neon signs indicating the Williams Walk would be great ideas.

Graham begs to differ. 'This would be self-defeating, and at the end of the day just who are you catering for? Such additions wouldn't enhance the place nor make it easier for people to walk round, but they would jar and spoil the aesthetics of Pukeiti. We've got to concentrate on the garden, make it more attractive for longer periods of the year. That really is our key.'[1]

Exceptions to this are flags outside the lodge with Dow Elanco, Taranaki Savings Bank, Easy 98 FM and Methanex on them. These are not seen as obtrusive because they are part of the flag system. Pukeiti is very careful with regard to sponsorship, advertising and other promotional links with business.

Another bone of contention is plant labelling. Some people want every plant named, while others complain of being unable to read what is already there. Either the name has faded, or lichen is eating into the paint — a peculiarity of Pukeiti's site and climate. However, Pukeiti believes it has got the balance right in this regard. Too many plant labels and the place would give the impression of a graveyard, which is also the reason why they are green and not white.

Surprisingly, donations are another touchy subject. Seating, for example, has quadrupled since Pukeiti was first opened. People often wish to donate a seat. Once again, aesthetics come into the picture. Where are the seats to be sited? There is also the cost of maintenance and other practicalities to consider. It is always a balancing act.

The Founders' Garden

An historic event in connection with the Founders' Garden occurred on 2 November 1996. This was the presenting and receiving of three carved Maori panels to commemorate the work of the original 25 founding members.

The feature, Te Whare Taonga, or the House of Treasures, is focused on three carved Maori panels set beneath a glass-roofed structure. This is sited below the main gatehouse entrance to the gardens. A dawn blessing by the representatives of the region's iwi preceded the afternoon ceremony. It was attended by an estimated 200 people.

John McIntyre, Pukeiti life member and co-ordinator of the project, described it as a very special moment. 'Even Pukeiti's birdlife seemed to realise the significance. The birds produced a magnificent dawn chorus.'[2]

Te Ru Wharehoka was the tohunga at the ceremony and a blessing was also delivered by Sir Paul Reeves and Stratford parson Reverend Tiki Raumati. Among the guests were Lady Mary Matthews and Pukeiti patron Ron Gordon, two of the four founding members still alive.

Above: Graham Smith with Governor-General Sir Michael Hardie Boys and Lady Hardie Boys.

Left: A working bee dead-heading on the Williams Walk. From left to right: Adrianne Downes, Heather Allan and Elsie Smith.

Above: The lodge.

Left: A rarely seen view of Pukeiti's beautiful and diverse native bush, including rimu, tree ferns and tawa.

The best part of 15 years of planning and preparation lay behind the unveiling. A semi-circle of golden fern pongas not usually found at Pukeiti, were planted in the late 1980s in preparation for the memorial. Wood for carvings was sourced at an early stage. The 600-year-old totara timber is from the Turangi Plateau and was given to Stratford carver, the late Robin Mason, by Maori from that area in 1982 for a special carving project.

Pukeiti Trust representatives, including John McIntyre, went to the Rangimarie Maori Arts and Crafts Centre. Chief carver Rangi Bailey and head bone carver Teimi Ahu, along with their students, took on the task of designing and carving the totara. The Maori story of creation was the subject chosen and the carvings have been done in the rare Taranaki style.

The carvings themselves had an immediate impact on hundreds of visitors to the Taranaki Rhododendron Festival that weekend. Someone was heard to comment that they looked as if they had been there forever.

Pukeiti's early Maori history is not well documented. However, it is known that the western and northern faces of the Kaitake and Pouakai ranges were dotted with small pa, summer camps and tracks. The Maori prophet Te Whiti O Rongamai from Parihaka is well connected to the area. His name is recorded in the Puketewhiti Stream, and previously the eastern spur of Pukeiti Hill was known as Puketewhiti.

During the late 1940s, the Te Kotahitanga Taurora Society purchased the lease of the west coast sector of Pukeiti, and that area north of Pukeiti Hill up to the Oakura River. Set up as a joint Maori-European society, it had plans to develop the area as a living model of the best of both cultures. Ideas of marae, model pa, camps, farms and retreats were put forward. Two youth hostels were built close to Carrington Road. 'Taitamahoa', the hostel of St Mary's Young People's Club, was dedicated by the Rt Rev. J.T. Holland, Bishop of Waikato, in 1955. Unfortunately the Society did not last long, and by 1958 all of this property was taken over by Pukeiti.

Opposite: Te Whare Taonga
unveiling ceremony, dawn, Saturday
2 November 1996. On the right is
Mrs Matarena Rau-Kupa, Kaumatua,
Kuia of the Ngati Mutunga tribe. On
her left is her niece, Mrs Ngaropi
Dianne Cameron.

Shelter belts, two buildings, farm clearings and tracks have been a legacy of this era. Only the buildings' foundations remain to this day.

The future — its dilemmas and challenges

The matter of funding is seen as a continuing dilemma and challenge rolled into one. Should Pukeiti remain privately funded, with its freedom and frugality, or seek government assistance, complete with strings attached? Both are seen to have good and bad points. Kew Gardens in the United Kingdom had been government-funded until recently, but are now having to go their own way. This necessitates the curator spending part of his time talking to wealthy Americans in an effort to rustle up funds.

Wisley Gardens, also in the United Kingdom, has by contrast been run as an enormous commercial enterprise for some time. They sell millions of pounds worth of books, plants and associated paraphernalia every year. They also run a training school and employ several hundred people. Britain's population base of over 50 million people allows for this. New Zealand's population is minuscule by comparison.

Government or council funding would give a sense of security and regular income, but the conditions attached and loss of independence were seen as too high a price to pay. Director Graham Smith recalled his disappointment after a recent trip back to the Royal Parks in London. 'The people I originally worked with were all dedicated plants people. They loved their plants and passed all that information on to you. It was something rather special. Today they've all gone over to contract and now it's just a job, like sweeping the roads or whatever. People don't have their souls in it any more. Pukeiti just couldn't work like that.'[3]

Pukeiti is not averse to developing business partnerships, but they need to be quite narrowly focused. Concessions include some use of the gardens, also Gold, Silver and Bronze sponsorships, which in return for a set annual cost provide a range of benefits and privileges for the sponsor. This can include guest passes to the garden, use of conference facilities and the display of the company logo at Pukeiti and in certain publications. Encouraging people to leave Pukeiti some money in their wills is another avenue of revenue. Donators usually ask if Pukeiti will remain as it is. They want to be sure that it is not going to turn into a theme park, for instance.

Computers have arrived on the scene to service business requirements and other purposes. A full database of plants is already underway, and making this available on the Internet and other international connections is now becoming a reality. Pukeiti and its storehouse of information will be more readily accessible to a wider range of users.

Buildings, or the lack of them, are presenting some problems for the Trust. Twenty years ago Graham Smith put forward a plan for a concrete-block building, to be constructed away from the public area. This was to house the workshop, poison store, staff messroom and a garden office. To date this has still not been erected.

The Board and Executive have not remained static in recent times. A series of resignations occurred in 1994. Differences of opinion on how the gardens should be managed were a key factor. The basic philosophical debate was between the purist gardeners and the business people responsible for turning Pukeiti around from its grim financial situation. Board chairman Peter Morpeth expressed disappointment at the loss of those who resigned, but he firmly believes that Pukeiti has a bright future.

Following on from this, the Board and Executive, each consisting of up to 15 people, have been replaced by one Board of 12. Seven board members come from within the Taranaki area, and five from beyond. The new board has formed a Members' Committee, thus ensuring that all members have access to board policy and other matters.

Graham Smith has been made Director of Pukeiti, responsible for all of its operations. Grant Carroll has been appointed Business Manager to supervise all the non-horticultural activities at Pukeiti. He is responsible to the Director. An appointment of Horticultural Curator, also responsible to the Director, has yet to be made. Karen Davis currently manages the Gatehouse.

The last word goes to Director Graham Smith, reflecting on Pukeiti's future. 'At the moment we're looking to 2001 when we'll be 50 years old. A big celebration is being planned. Then we have to think to 2050. Where will we be at? This place is so much more than just individuals. It's growing all the time in reputation, and we have the responsibility for ensuring that it is passed on intact to future generations.'[4]

Above: Ron Gordon, Founding Member, past Board Chairman and Patron. Pukeiti

Opposite: The New Plymouth Pipe Band playing on the main lawn during the 1995 Taranaki Rhododendron Festival.

Pukeiti's Flora & Fauna

by Graham Smith, Director

CHAPTER SIX

The rhododendron collection

Douglas Cook bought the 63 hectares of Pukeiti Hill because he thought it was the ideal place to grow rhododendrons. The location also gives Pukeiti its uniqueness and vibrancy. No other major garden in the world is set amidst a natural temperate rainforest.

The soil has a pH of 5.5 or lower in most parts. Because the topography is rugged, some areas are wetter and cooler than the sunny north-facing slopes and ridges. The high rainfall, evenly spread throughout the year, ensures many plants luxuriate in these conditions. Equally, others turn up their toes within days of arrival. There is a steep learning curve as to what will or will not grow at Pukeiti. The rainfall, competition from native plants, predation by animals, insects and disease, have all contributed to the success or otherwise of many plant introductions.

It was considered in the early days that Pukeiti's isolation would keep it free of 'nasties'. No such luck! Certainly, the climate is against the establishment of some pests and diseases, but it is equally encouraging for others. Vigilance by staff and the correct use of quarantine facilities are the main line of defence.

Back in 1951, the Founder Members and volunteers worked in good faith. They committed £450 (a lot of money then) to ordering a consignment of rhododendron plants from the United Kingdom which set the collection on its way. These duly arrived by air, and were briefly quarantined by a local nursery free of charge. This set the pattern for many years, when almost all services were supplied free of charge or in kind.

Those formative years were very hectic as word spread about Pukeiti and what was being achieved. Douglas Cook sent over a vast number of plants from his Eastwoodhill garden, or organised seed from his many friends overseas. Russell Matthews used his influence to raise money and his presence to get workers on site. These two men, coupled with the quiet authority of plantsman John Goodwin, were the motivators that saw the uniqueness of Pukeiti unfold into reality. It was they who promoted a vote of £25 to Frank Kingdon Ward's last major expedition to Burma in 1953.

In the same year, another large consignment of rhododendrons arrived from the United Kingdom, prompting the realisation that a nursery area was needed to house all this new material before it was ready to plant. The lodge was being built and a future lawn was planned to be laid out in front of it. What better use beforehand than as a stock nursery? By 1955, more than 500 rhododendrons, 380 trees and shrubs and 340 native species were lined out.

Left: Andrew Brooker (left) and Peter Davis standing next to R. protistum *var.* giganteum.

Previous page left: R. 'Hollard No.9' growing in the Stead Block.

Previous page right: The two ponds on the Matthews Walk. Plants featured around the pond include Acer palmatum *'Dissectum Atropurpureum', Glen Dale azaleas, primulas, cardiocrinums, tree ferns and* Gunnera tinctoria.

The flowers of R. grande, *one of Pukeiti's resplendent large-leafed rhododendrons.*

The year 1955 must have been a busy one, because more than 20 packets of rhododendron seed arrived from Scotland and 48 packets of the same from Frank Knight at Wisley in the United Kingdom. James Russell, also in the United Kingdom, sent 44 packets of primula seed. In addition, 177 rhododendron plants, all species, were given by Les Taylor of Stratford, plus 50 *Kalmia latifolia* from Ron Duncan. The first large-leafed rhododendron, *R. sinogrande*, was planted, and the Hybrid Block saw its first planting. Never mind that they were all blown out of the ground soon afterwards — the garden was under way! (The early members were so enthusiastic, they didn't realise that by clearing the Hybrid Block of everything, they let the wind in.)

The general idea was to gather as much plant material as was available in the nursery industry which might be suitable for trial. Duncan & Davies's nursery played an important part in this. Whilst large purchases were made, even larger gifts were received. This was typical of the generosity of plants people, and I am pleased to say that it still continues today.

Modern nursery people, many seeking out new plants from the wild like Os Blumhardt, Mark Jury, Glyn Church, Bill Robinson and Dennis Hughes, all share good things with Pukeiti. Much of this comes from establishing your name. There is no doubt this is what was done so well in those early days.

John Goodwin visited the United Kingdom in 1957. Through his connections he was able to visit many private gardens and obtain seed from these of rare rhododendrons and other shrubs. It was also the year that George Huthnance, one of the best rhododendron nurserymen in New Zealand, passed on more than 300 new plants, propagated from imported cuttings and scions. Many of these can be seen in the garden today as mature specimens. Their offspring have spread far and wide throughout New Zealand.

The year 1960 was another extremely busy one, with extensive plantings being carried out in all areas. More than 150 rhododendron hybrids, 100 species, 200 deciduous azaleas, 147 evergreen azaleas and 1300 bulbs were planted. It was also the first time a Vireya rhododendron appeared on the list — *R. gracilentum,* sent over from Papua New Guinea by the then chief botanist, John Womersley of Lae Botanical Gardens. Unfortunately it did not survive, but the connection did, as I was able to meet John at Pukeiti in 1983. This led to two plant-hunting expeditions to Papua New Guinea. From these the Vireya rhododendron collection expanded to become one of the best in the world.

One interesting entry in the 'Plant Inwards' records for 1960 was a donation of seed from Douglas Cook — *Cannabis sativa*! Against it, in brackets, it said 'Hemp'. In those early days of innocence, cannabis was grown quite extensively for its excellent fibre qualities, producing hemp for rope-making. I am sure it never took off commercially at Pukeiti. The authorities today would take a very dim view if I tried to reintroduce this aromatic herb to our summer borders!

The pace of development slowed in the 1960s as areas of the garden were planted, and consolidation took over. The decade was notable, however, for the planting of the Valley of the Giants. This was a steep-sided, sheltered valley, almost horseshoe in shape. The mostly aging kamahi forest was felled to give light and space. The

Above: R. 'Winsome', *growing close to the lodge, with an attendant bumble bee.*

Opposite: R. 'Noyo Chief'. *Pukeiti's 'wet light' brings the dazzling colours to life.*

idea was to emulate a Himalayan valley, and have the large-leafed rhododendrons looking like they had always been there. Today that is exactly what the effect is. Self-sown seedlings are now thrusting up under their parents to provide another generation, thus achieving the original vision of Rob Hair.

Prior to 1963, another notable event took place. That was the planting or sowing of seed of the giant Himalayan lily, *Cardiocrinum giganteum*. It was brought from Gwavas, the Hawke's Bay garden of Foundation Member Michael Hudson, and scattered along the margins of walks. Seed had been distributed about the bush margins before this, but its success rate was unrecorded. Today, *Cardiocrinum* are one of the great features in the garden at Christmas time. Hundreds of 2-4 metre stems carry huge, richly-scented, white trumpet flowers. Because the plant seeds so freely, some stems are cut down before they ripen. These are then dried off to be sold for flower arranging. The seed is destroyed, and measures are taken to keep the plants within the garden proper.

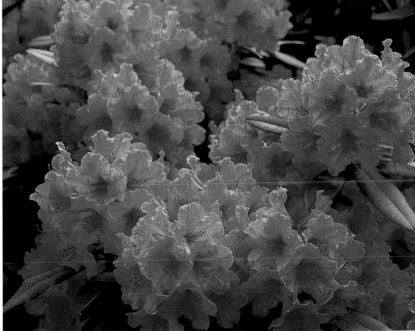

There is a fine balance between a successful planting and the creation of a plant nuisance. The introduction of new plants is usually an exciting prospect, with the fears mostly being set towards survival. Occasionally the opposite happens and a choice plant becomes a problem.

A case in point is the Chilean flame creeper, *Tropaeolum speciosum*. What a wonderful scarlet-flowered climber this is! However, the roots go down as far as the plant goes up. It totally smothers trees and shrubs, remains evergreen and can kill out its host. In a word, it is a 'menace' which we are unable to get rid of. We are now very circumspect in the introduction of new plants, ensuring precautions are in place so that rogues can be destroyed.

The 1970s brought a fresh surge in the importation of new plants, much of it as a result of visits to the United Kingdom and United States. Famous gardens such as Exbury, Wisley, Savill and Brodick were the sources of many fine new rhododendron hybrids, plus some valuable named forms of species.

Was it sheer coincidence, or did we know something? The 1980s were the busiest time for introducing new plants, particularly from the wild, that we had seen. Pukeiti members became involved with plant explorations in many parts of the world. The fruits of their labours continue to enhance Pukeiti's image.

Keith Adams, a noted plant hunter, went off the beaten track in Borneo to such places as Gunong Mulu, Bukit Lumut and Batu Lawei in his search for tropical Vireyas. Keith first started plant-hunting in 1980, and since then has racked up more than nine trips to this part of the world. He is so well known in 'his' part of Sarawak that he has been adopted by an Iban longhouse and given the tribal name 'Kadam' — a corruption of Keith and Adams. Blood-sucking leeches (Keith has a horror of them) and lunatic drivers ensure that 'been there, done that' touristy types shy away from such places. Keith often gets asked if he uses Dimp in the jungle to repel mosquitoes. He just laughs and replies that this gets sweated off within five minutes, and is about as useful as a cellphone in a cave!

Above: R. javanicum *var.* brookeanum *in the Perrott Glasshouse. This Vireya comes from Mt Kinabalu, Borneo.*

Left: R. rubineiflorum *growing in the Covered Walk. This is one of the smallest rhododendrons in the world, the plant label gives some indication of its size.*

Below left: Keith Adams, plant hunter, with an array of hats from Borneo and wearing a necklace made from boars' tusks given to him by the Tarago people of the Borneo highlands.

On one occasion Keith brought back a particular *R. lanceolatum* which was found to be new to cultivation. It is discoveries like that which make all the privations worthwhile. Aside from this, Keith disclosed that his most remarkable experience was not the discovery of a new plant, but the witnessing of about one million bats emerging from their daytime roosts in Deer Cave. 'They were spiralling up like a giant water-spout. We were incredibly lucky because they were going past us to feed on fruit that night. The next night they might have been going in another direction. I've never seen anything like it before or since,' Keith marvelled.

Alan Jellyman made numerous trips to uncharted areas in Nepal, and I have collected in Papua New Guinea, Malaysia and China. Other friends of Pukeiti also add to the plant richness, such as Peter Cox from Scotland, who sends seed from all his expeditions, mainly in China. Not since the 1920s and 1930s has so much exploration been done.

In recent years an emphasis has been placed on extending the season of interest, in line with Pukeiti's logo and motto 'A Garden for all Seasons'. Certainly, building up the Vireya rhododendron collection has enhanced this. Their flowering covers every month of the year, with peaks during late winter and early summer. Out in the gardens, the summer borders which developed from the spring displays of primulas, hostas and meconopsis, down each side of the main drive have been considerably enlarged. They now form the garden's entrance. With a careful selection of plants, colour is achieved over eight months of the year.

Trees and shrubs to complement the rhododendron collection have been a priority from day one. Many, particularly deciduous species, have been tried. Unfortunately, a large number have failed for various reasons. This is an evergreen rainforest, and a number of plants we associate with 'woodland gardening' do not thrive here. You will not see many Japanese maples, cherries, birches, dogwoods, mountain ash or oaks. However, the climate is conducive to hydrangeas, which are now planted in their hundreds to give wonderful summer colour.

Dimorphanthera alpina, *a rare rhododendron relative from Papua New Guinea on display in the Covered Walk.*

Below: R. '*Gardenia Odessey*' *flowering for the first time in 1995 in the Covered Walk. This plant has a beautiful perfume.*

For many people a walk in the bush on a hot summer's day is a joy in itself. We have to keep reminding ourselves of the importance of this aspect of Pukeiti. If I had to pick my favourite spot, it would be the water-wheel and dam — for its cool greenness, sounds of water, birds singing and trout lazing in the shallows. I think the Creator, with a little help from Man, got this just right — paradise on earth!

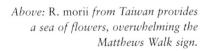

Above: R. morii *from Taiwan provides a sea of flowers, overwhelming the Matthews Walk sign.*

Right: R. macabeanum *x* 'Pamela' *is a lovely hybrid growing in the Stead Block.*

Far right: Vireya rhododendron R. superbum, collected by Graham Smith in Papua New Guinea in 1983.

The original aim of Pukeiti was to gather as many of the superior and award-winning rhododendrons as was possible, mainly by importing them from the United Kingdom. These would complement what was already available in New Zealand, and illustrate the advance in breeding being done overseas.

Large-leafed rhododendrons, the giants of the race, were always a priority because hardly any were being grown here at the time. In fact few gardens anywhere in the world specialised in the 'big leafs' — members of the Grandia and Falconera sections. They were to form the basis of a collection of the more tender species. How right that judgement has been. Forty-five years since the project began, Pukeiti now grows one of the world's most important collections of warm temperate and tropical rhododendron species.

Pukeiti's so-called 'perfect conditions' have to be put into perspective, and recognition given that there can be no such thing. Rhododendrons generally grow in elevated regions of the Northern Hemisphere, where there is ample moisture in late spring and summer to encourage growth, also a drying period in late summer to ripen wood and set flowerbuds. This very simplistic statement cannot cover every variation of habitat, which can range from Florida sand dunes to fissures in granite rock on ice-capped tropical mountains in Borneo.

The driest period for many rhododendrons in the wild is winter — the exact opposite of conditions prevailing at Pukeiti. Wet, cool winters are not liked by plants that are programmed to being in virtual hibernation for many months, protected by snow or in a dry atmosphere. Not for us the high-elevation alpine *Lapponica*, the fine-foliaged *Taliensia*, or the acute-drainage-requiring *Neriiflora* — or at least not in major plantings. Having said that, the challenge is hard to resist, and we try to maintain some of these difficult plants in our collection. However, unless they are good garden plants, they fail to do justice to the value of the rhododendron genus as a whole and are removed.

Large-leafed rhododendrons

The large-leafed rhododendrons tend to flower early in the season, from mid winter to mid spring, and also make their growth early. For this reason they require shelter from anything but light frosts, wind protection, and a lot of moisture to support their substantial foliage and frame. They also grow tree-like in many species and so need a lot of room. Pukeiti fulfils all these requirements admirably.

All of the earliest plantings came from seed-grown plants, with seed coming from both New Zealand and United Kingdom sources. A lot turned out to be hybrids, but nonetheless they are extremely handsome and excitingly floriferous plants. Some notable hybrid seed was obtained from Glenarn Gardens in Scotland. These have produced fine-foliaged plants. One outstanding yellow, now called 'Falcon's Gold', was raised from *R. falconeri* and *R. macabeanum*.

New growth of a large-leafed rhododendron seedling, R. magnificum x macabeanum.

The most notable and exciting introduction of this early period was Frank Kingdon Ward's KW 21498 seed from The Triangle, northeast Burma, collected in 1953 as 'Grande series?'. Three seedlings were planted close to our Giant Rata, and the first flowering on two of them was in 1974. They caused a sensation because of their sheer size and rich pink colouring. One stayed this colour while the other paled quickly as it aged. The latter plant died while the other grew bigger and better each year. This is identified as *R. protistum var. giganteum*. Because of its superior quality and value to the garden, it has been registered simply as 'Pukeiti'. This has become a bit of a celebrity in the rhododendron world. Now more than 12 metres in diameter, each July and August it regularly produces 100-200 trusses, the size of soccer balls.

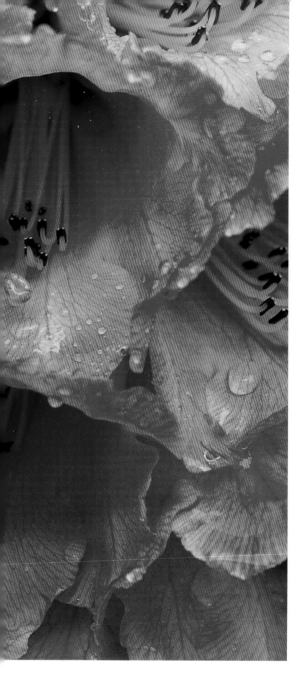

The third seedling grew very upright and did not flower until 1990. It is a superb form as well, and looks destined to reach the incredible 30-metre heights recorded in China and Burma. Seedlings have since been raised from these two forms.

More recently, another collection was made of this species in southwest Yunnan, from the trees first recorded by George Forrest in 1919. Pukeiti was able to obtain seed from this collection in 1991. It now has a considerable number of young plants waiting to be planted out. The thought of a whole valley of this species in flower is very exciting, even if it could be 2012 before they bloom!

Many other big-leaf species are grown, including *R. protistum*'s close cousin, *R. magnificum*, from the same region. This has rose-purple-coloured flowers. *R. grande* from the Himalayas, and *R. sinogrande* from Yunnan, China, are well represented, including more recently collected seed from the wild.

Above: The flowers of R. protistum giganteum *var. 'Pukeiti', the symbol of the Pukeiti Rhododendron Trust. At right, this magnificent rhododendron is shown in a bush setting with the Giant Rata looming high above it.*

Top right: R. macabeanum, *a large-leafed species rhododendron.*

The beauty of R. maddenii, *flowering to perfection on the main lawn, is enhanced by a spider's web flecked with raindrops. This rhododendron has a sweet, languid perfume.*

R. macabeanum has attractive creamy-yellow flowers, sometimes with a deep maroon blotch. All our plants are grown from garden-raised seed and may be hybridised. The same applies to plants of *R. rex, praestans, montroseanum, basilicum, falconeri, arizelum* and *fictolacteum.*

Recent collections in the wild by members and friends of Pukeiti have yielded stock of *R. hodgsonii,* the newly named *R. kesangiae,* also *R. sinofalconeri, falconeri* and *fictolacteum,* to give us a good base for another generation of planting. All produce magnificent foliage plants, whether they are hybrids or true species, and for 12 months of the year they give enormous satisfaction as superb rainforest specimens.

The Maddenias

The Maddenias are another group of somewhat tender rhododendrons that thrive at Pukeiti. These are trumpet-flowered, scented rhododendrons that are typified by the popular nursery plant *R.* 'Fragrantissimum', a very old English hybrid. Maddenias are typically compact, bushy shrubs. In the wild they are often epiphytic, growing on rocks, stumps, or up in the tops of trees. Many flower and make growth early in the season, and as such are susceptible to hard frosts. The flowers are predominantly white and funnel- or trumpet-shaped. The scents are as varied as the plants themselves, which often have wonderful polished or flaky mahogany-coloured bark. They also range from compact, bushy plants only 50 cm tall to open trees of up to 10 metres.

As a group, Maddenias are somewhat difficult to sort out, and even the experts disagree. Thankfully, recent name changes have simplified the matter, but with so many forms and varieties being grown over many years, the origins of these are somewhat obscured. Pukeiti imported many Maddenia species in the 1970s and 1980s to try to sort out some of the confusion, but there is a limited range in the United Kingdom because so many have to be grown under glass.

Once again, seed from Frank Kingdon Ward's expeditions in 1950 and 1953 have produced some outstanding plants. One, a beautiful pink with a deeper throat that has masqueraded under the *R. ciliicalyx* label for a long time, we now call 'Charisma'. It is wonderfully fragrant and has a relatively compact habit. The other is a form of *R. maddenii* subs. *crassum*, which flowers near Christmas time and has exceptionally large white trumpet flowers. The foliage is also outstanding. This was imported from Brodick Castle Gardens on the Isle of Arran, Scotland, where a fine range of these plants are grown in mild conditions. Another island garden, Gigha, provided more choice species, including the 'yellow polyandrum'. We call this very fine plant 'Yellow Dawn' because it is so distinctive.

The most handsome of all of this group of rhododendrons has to be *R. nuttallii*. It makes a small tree and has wonderful smooth reddish bark. The flowers are really something else — the largest of the genus, bar a few Vireyas. White trumpets, flushed red on the tube, make for an impressive sight. Each truss can have up to 12 flowers, spaced like spokes of a wheel — an aristocrat in every way.

The Maddenias, like the big-leafs, are so happy at Pukeiti that they are self-seeding in large numbers. One or two good hybrids have been put aside for further assessment.

Above: R. 'Seven Stars' can be seen just below the main lawn on the way to the pond.

Left: The flowers of R. sinogrande, another beautiful large-leafed rhododendron.

Vireyas

The importance of Vireya rhododendrons to Pukeiti cannot be over-stated. They are flamboyant, easy to grow and easy to propagate. From a visitor point of view they have tremendous impact and educational value.

The entrance to the original Display House had a plant of *R.* 'Simbu Sunset' beside it. This hybrid between two Papua New Guinea species, *R. laetum* and *R. zoelleri*, was raised and named at Pukeiti. A spectacular plant, it produces large vivid orange and yel-low flowers in a number of bursts throughout the year, and never fails to arouse comment. Many people started growing Vireyas after having seen *R.* 'Simbu Sunset'.

The Pukeiti collection features a few very old hybrids, plus many developed over the past 20 years. These include Pukeiti-raised ones such as 'Java Light', 'Flamenco Dancer', 'Silken Shimmer' and 'Fireflash'.

Other rhododendrons

The rest of the rhododendron collection is no less important. With about 2500 different specimens, there is plenty of interest and diversity. For example, *R. yakushimanum*, one of the most popular and sought after rhododendrons in the world, is grown to perfection at Pukeiti. Imported from England in 1952, a massive plant (one of two) growing on the lawn ridge is thought to be one of the largest in cultivation. In 1974 the smaller version was replanted, due to being overcrowded by its vigorous companion. The *yakushimanum* 'junior' was moved once again in September 1978 to the main entrance gates. There it remains to the present day.

More important, from a botanical viewpoint, is the comprehensive collection of species, many of which have been sourced from the wild. Some species such as *R. stamineum*, *ciliipes*, *vialii*, *subansiriense* and *excellens* are quite rare. Many have never been seen in New Zealand before, or indeed other countries, and it has been exciting to watch them mature. In some cases, this has been the first opportunity to add to the written record that forms an important part of Pukeiti's function.

A special area is devoted to New Zealand-raised hybrids, and excellent work has been done by local plant breeders, particularly with regards to the warmer-climate rhododendrons, these being better suited to temperate conditions, rather than those of colder countries. Pukeiti also has raised and registered a number of hybrids, including the lovely pale yellow 'Lemon Lodge', apricot-cream 'Spiced Honey', pink and cream 'Ina Hair', deep red 'Sir Russell Matthews', and the pink 'Satin Cloud'.

Work on the rhododendron collection never ceases. New material is coming to hand every season, and the influx of seed from many parts of the world ensures future plantings will continue at a steady rate. The warmer regions of southern China, Burma, Vietnam, Thailand and the Himalayas are yielding new or different forms of species. Hybridisers are forever seeking the perfect rhododendron. We keep planting their latest creations, knowing full well that next year they will come up with something better!

Opposite top: R. dalhousiae *var.* rhabdotum, *a late bloomer. This photograph was taken in January.*

Opposite below: R. elliottii *has magnificent red flowers, further enhanced by evening light.*

Right: R. 'Loder's White' *photographed in the Founders' Garden.*

Below left: R. 'Rubicon' *is a red hybrid bred by Pukeiti Foundation Member Ron Gordon.*

Below right: R. 'Babylon' *is a hybrid growing on the Ayckbourn Walk.*

Above: R. 'Lemon Lodge' seedling in the Stead Block.

Right: R. 'Lem's Cameo', a difficult rhododendron to propagate but one of the most spectacular when in full bloom.

CHAPTER SEVEN

Other flora and fauna at Pukeiti

Early plantings of traditional woodland trees and shrubs at Pukeiti showed promise, but the climate and possum depredation gradually reduced the number of these that were reliable.

Magnolias have been top of the list of companion plants. The first plantings of seedling *Magnolia campbellii* took off like rockets. Unfortunately, possums developed a taste for them, and it has been a real struggle ever since to get them established. The original trees are now big enough to look after themselves, and annually produce hundreds of huge pale pink or white blooms in September. The summer-flowering *M. sieboldii* and *M. globosa* have also done well. Their cup-shaped white flowers bloom over a couple of months. They also seed readily, and young plants appear in great profusion. The evergreen *M. grandiflora* and *M. delavayi* also grow well, but are not as vigorous as their cousin *Michelia doltsopa*. This magnificent evergreen tree thrives in the Pukeiti climate. A number of superb specimens are regularly smothered in highly scented, cream flowers from August to October. Recently we have planted a number of clones of *Michelia yunnanensis*. These show great promise.

Above: Cardiocrinum giganteum, *the giant Himalayan lily. This richly perfumed lilium is a real treasure over the Christmas period at Pukeiti and a favourite with visitors.*

Above right: The huge blooms of Magnolia grandiflora 'Goliath' *only last for one day.*

Below right: Michelia doltsopa, *complete with lichens and ferns.*

Various members of the Ericaceae family, close relatives of rhododendrons, naturally feature in the garden — *Pieris, Kalmia* and *Enkianthus*, one of the few really reliable genera for autumn colour in Pukeiti's climate. Other more unusual members of the family include *Craibiodendron yunnanense*, a tall evergreen shrub resembling *Pieris,* also several *Dimorphanthera* species from Papua New Guinea. *Agapetes* and *Vaccineum* are grown as epiphytes.

Stewartia and camellia belong to the same Theaceae family. Both are well represented. Although the stewartias are essentially deciduous, they do well, providing white flowers in mid summer and good autumn colour. The camellia collection concentrates on the more tender species and hybrids, leaving out *C. japonica*. Many new species have become available in New Zealand over the past 20 years, and we have endeavoured to try these out.

Clethras have done well, and again give useful colour and scent in mid to late summer. The deciduous species turn a bright yellow in autumn, but the real success is with the tender evergreen *Clethra arborea* from Madeira. It forms a vigorous, upright tree to 8 metres, has handsome foliage and flowers profusely. The cream lily-of-the-valley-like flowers are scented, and it self-seeds around the garden. We have just acquired *C. mexicana*, which is an extremely handsome foliaged plant. It shows great promise.

Opposite above: Magnolia campbellii.

Below: Hydrangea *'Hamburg'.*
Hydrangeas thrive at Pukeiti and
provide plenty of summer colour.

Right: The flowers of the beautiful
climber Tecomanthe montana *on*
display in the Covered Walk. All the
plants grown in New Zealand have
originated from this one specimen,
brought into the country from Papua
New Guinea by Graham Smith
in 1986.

Daphne bholua has been a wonderful introduction in recent years, and few people fail to notice it when in bloom. It has an upright habit, is evergreen in our climate, and forms dense thickets 2 to 3 metres tall. The flowering season is incredibly long — May to October — and the blossoms' intoxicating fragrance permeates over a wide area. Most of our plants have been grown from seed collected by Alan Jellyman in Nepal. We are now rewarded by plants self-seeding regularly.

Mention should be made of the fine specimen of *Philesia magellanica*. It was planted on a raised peat and tree-fern-fibre bed beside the original director's office in 1980, along with many other treasures like *Cassiope* and *Kalmiopsis*. Sixteen years later it covers 6 square metres. The deep pink waxy bells appear all summer and provoke a lot of comment.

Cornus, Styrax, Corylopsis, Deutzia, Philadelphus, Viburnum, Mahonia, Hamamelis and many other more common plants are grown, along with such rarities as *Trochodendron aralioides* and *Daphniphyllum humile*. Conifers are also used, but because many do not look aesthetically pleasing with the rainforest background, they are planted sparingly. *Cryptomeria japonica*, the Japanese cedar, relishes the conditions. It self-seeds readily and has withstood cyclonic winds that dropped others. Tsugas also enjoy the high rainfall and blend in well. Southern Hemisphere podocarps mimic their New Zealand cousins and make very handsome garden specimens, particularly *Podocarpus henkellii* and *P. salignus*. A collection of dwarf conifers is used around the lodge and main lawn to emphasise the space. Unfortunately, the word 'dwarf' is a misnomer in this climate, as most become large shrubs in a short period of time.

Herbaceous plants play an important role in the spring and summer scene, highlighting the rhododendron collection, then becoming a feature in their own right. The early season is dominated by thousands of candelabra primulas. Complementing these are Spanish bluebells, hostas, astilbes, rodgersias, omphalodes, trilliums and irises, all of which produce a wonderful spring display.

These are followed by traditional summer plants such as alchemilla, heliopsis, digitalis, helianthus, coreopsis, sedum, kniphofia, lobelia and chrysanthemum. The more unusual

meconopsis, hardy orchids such as *Pleione, Bletilla, Disa* and *Dactylorriza*, lilium species and arisaema, all add to the scene. Bulbous plants such as *Tigridia pavonia, Galtonia candicans*, rhodohypoxis, narcissus, crocus, crinum and colchicum, spread themselves right through the season, creating pools of colour and a lot of interest for the visitor.

Pukeiti is not just rhododendrons, but an amalgam of many different plants that thrive in the unusual conditions, all set within a modified rainforest environment. This has created something rather special, and can proudly be handed down as an example of what can be achieved when people work together, unselfishly, towards a common goal.

Above: Pink Astilbe *growing alongside the drive at Pukeiti.*

Right: Lilium nepalense *in the Founders' Garden. This species hails from the Himalayas and is not an easy subject to cultivate.*

The spectacular native climber Clematis paniculata.

Native flora and fauna

There is hesitation in calling the bush here 'natural', because it is not. Pukeiti has an almost totally modified forest canopy. These changes occurred even before the axe was heard throughout the forest, but were of a natural kind. Cyclical changes evolve over hundreds or thousands of years. Global warming, or cooling, droughts (often accompanied by fire), severe storms, and in Pukeiti's case, volcanic activity, have all contributed to the basic makeup.

People have hastened the natural processes considerably. The lowland mountain rainforest mix was dominated by the rimu (*Dacrydium cupressinum*) and rata (*Metrosideros robusta*). However, by the turn of the century, the rata was already in decline for whatever reason, and the rimu was about to be milled.

In 1868, the search for building materials coincided with the formation of the Egmont National Park, first in 1875 as a forest reserve, then in 1901 as a national park. Because of this, only privately owned land could be milled in this vicinity. In 1922, the New Plymouth Sash & Door Company established a mill at the top of Kirihau Road. A tramline was laid up the right bank of Momona Stream, with hauler lines converging from the area to the south and east. Horses were used to haul logs out of the bush and along the line to the mill. The stream was bridged in 1923, and by 1926 a Fordson Nattrass tractor replaced the horses. By this time the line had reached the Oakura River.

Top: The native daisy Brachyglottis kirkii *full of fluffy seed, ready to disperse in the wind.*

Above: Brachyglottis kirkii *again, this time smothered with flowers. It is an epiphyte and can be found perching in trees and on stumps.*

Left: This is believed to be Fomitopsis hemitephra, *a fungus found on native hardwoods. This specimen is approximately 60 centimetres across.*

By 1928, two Robertson steam haulers were in use, one at the mill, the other along the line. Some of the excavated hauler lines were up to a kilometre in length.

Country immediately to the north of Trig Pukeiti was owned by Pouakai Minerals Ltd. For a number of years they had been extracting iron-oxide ore from a group of pits known as the 'paint mines'. During the early 1920s, the ore was taken up Saxtons Track (a partly formed section of Surrey Hill Road), to Saxtons Hut on Carrington Road. Packhorses were used. After the tramline had reached the Oakura River in 1926, an agreement was made between Sash & Door and Pouakai Minerals. In exchange for timber extraction rights, the milling company agreed to take the line to the paint mines. That line continued as far as the hauler station, not far from the present Pukeiti lodge.

By 1931, all millable timber in the area over which the Sash & Door Company had rights had been extracted. The bridges were dismantled and the imported Oregon timber recovered from the larger ones. (Small bridges had been built with indigenous timber such as pukatea and hinau, which did not last long and rotted easily.)

This action had all but decimated the forest, as other valuable timber trees were also taken. Firewood cutters administered the final *coup de grâce* when they came in and removed the hardwoods. Very little original bush remained, as damp, humid shade was replaced by open scrub – conditions favoured by goats and possums. They ensured that regrowth was kept to a minimum, and was restricted to less palatable species.

The largest moss in the world,
Dawsonia superba.

*Left: The Poor Knights Lily
(*Xeronema callistemon*) growing in
the Covered Walk. One specimen also
grows outside on a large log. This
species originates from the Poor
Knights Islands just off the
Whangarei coast. It requires excellent
drainage and can be slow to flower,
but the wait is worth it.*

*Below: The shining rata or akakura
(*Metrosideros fulgens*). This climbing
vine flowers from February through
to July.*

Top: Mahoe or whiteywood (Melicytus ramiflorus) *is a common native shrub at Pukeiti. Also seen are the seed pods of the giant Himalayan lily.*

Above: Even in death, this huge rata has a certain majesty about it.

When the Trust was formed, Pukeiti was covered with a mix of evergreen saplings. Some were 30 to 40 years old, with the occasional large tree standing clear of the canopy.

Many young tree seedlings live in a state of almost suspended animation in a normal forest situation. They grow minute amounts in their dark environment, awaiting the day when an old tree falls and a pocket of light appears. They will then take off, vying for the position of number one, and eventually taking their place in the forest canopy. In a modified forest, quick-growing species can overwhelm slower ones, preventing the likes of rimu from developing.

On Pukeiti's land a programme of pest control, combined with release clearing of the slower-growing podocarps, was the first stage of recovery. This was enhanced by a replanting programme, particularly of rimu, to restore some balance. Most were planted along track and road margins so that they could be monitored and admired by all as they grew. Forty years on, the largest of these are now beautiful trees. This type of planting does not stop, and every winter another 50 or 100 saplings are put out in a continuation of the programme.

The main components of this evergreen rainforest are extremely diverse. They give the bush its characteristic blend of form and varying shades of green. Rimu stands out because of the light green strands of weeping, coarse stems that have been likened to 'green rain'. In the young state it is an elegant, pyramidal tree, varying considerably from seedling to seedling. An aged specimen is craggy-topped with a massive trunk, soaring up to 30-40 metres.

Rata, on the other hand, starts its life high up in the canopy of an old tree, usually rimu, and sends roots down to the ground. These thicken with age, and eventually take over from the host tree which dies out. What is left is usually a cylindrical massive trunk of joined aerial roots, topped off by a head of dark foliage. In some years a mass of red flowers are produced.

The Giant Rata is Pukeiti's prime specimen and is estimated to be over 800 years old. Its sheer size probably spared it from the firewood cutters. Of all the native hardwoods, this burns the best. Unlike the rimu, the wood has little commercial value, save for turning on a lathe. Sadly, this tree, like most of its surviving generation, is dying, victim to old age and possum predation. Even sadder is that there are few replacements.

Three trees make up the major canopy of Pukeiti today. They are tawa, hinau and kamahi. Tawa (*Beilschmiedia tawa*) is a handsome specimen with a straight, smooth, dark trunk. It has a massive crown of branches supporting pale green, almost translucent, willow-like leaves. The tiny flowers give way to large, date-like purple fruits which form an important part of the diet of large birds, possums and rats. A typical specimen will also support a community of epiphytic plants, ranging from huge clumps of astelia to tiny *Drymoanthus* orchids.

Hinau (*Elaeocarpus dentatus*) has a distinctive juvenile phase like so many New Zealand plants. When young, it is a thick whippy specimen with long, narrow-toothed leaves. With age it becomes a straight-trunked tree carrying a large head of upward-pointing branches. The glossy leaves are narrow and smooth. It produces handsome cream flowers in panicles in early summer, so thick that the bush can change colour.

*Above: Kiekie (*Freycinetia*) colonising a dead tree trunk.*

*Left: The white rata (*Metrosideros perforata*), a small-leafed native climber that flowers in February.*

Kamahi (*Weinmannia racemosa*) is a relatively quick-growing, small-leafed tree that has colonised Pukeiti since the rimu was felled. Some very old specimens, short trunked with a wide spreading crown, are found as remnants of the early forest. Most of the young trees are upright. The new growth has a reddish tinge and when in bloom the spikes of tiny white flowers, much loved by bees, smother the trees. These are followed by reddish seed capsules which again change the look of the bush. Possums find kamahi to their liking and can inflict severe damage.

A number of other trees tend to form isolated specimens or groups within the main canopy. These include rewarewa (*Knightia excelsa*), a most distinctive upright tree with long, coarsely toothed leaves. It has unusual dark-red, spidery flowers like its close cousin, *Grevillea*. It produces plenty of nectar and bees make distinctive

honey from it. The wood is wonderfully mottled and is used in furniture making.

Pukatea (*Laurelia novae-zelandiae*) grows tall and straight. Like its tropical relatives, it produces plank buttresses at the base. Glossy, bright green, oblong leaves form a distinctive head to the tree. It loves moist ground and avoids the drier ridges.

Miro (*Prumnopitys ferruginea*) is the most common of the podocarps (southern conifers) at Pukeiti. The very dense, yew-like foliage sets it apart from everything else. It survives well in sun or deep shade. It is readily spread by native pigeons who gorge themselves silly on the succulent red fruit, which smell strongly of turpentine. Large old trees are rare, but can reach 25 metres with straight, black, hammer-marked trunks.

One of the most distinctive of all trees at Pukeiti is the lancewood

(*Pseudopanax crassifolius*), which in its juvenile form has to be the oddest plant. A single, thin stem with rigid, dark green, sword-like leaves up to 30 cm long, reaches up to 4 or 5 metres. Having reached this height, the plant begins to branch out. At the same time the leaves are reduced in length, but become wider, like those of a normal tree. Having thus moved into the adult stage, it becomes a round-topped tree with a thick, deeply grooved trunk.

Almost everything in the forest is evergreen, but one tree or shrub stands out for dropping all of its leaves in winter, *Fuchsia excorticata* or kotukutuku. It also has the most distinctive flaking, peeling bark of the palest tan colour which stands out vividly amongst everything else. The grey-backed leaves are translucent in the sun, and the purple, red and green flowers are only clearly seen when the sun shines through them. Bellbirds and tuis can frequently be seen working their way up and down the stems, sipping nectar from every bell.

There is a large range of shrubby plants that fill in the under-storey at Pukeiti, providing cover and food for many birds. These include mahoe (*Melicytus ramiflorus*), five finger (*Neopanax arboreum*), *Coprosma* spp., hangehange (*Geniostoma ligustrifolium*), pate (*Schefflera digitata*), horopito (*Pseudowintera axillaris*), wineberry (*Aristotelia serrata*), and pigeonwood (*Hedycarya arborea*).

Growing amongst these are a number of climbers and vines which give the forest a lush, well furnished look. Most prominent at certain seasons are the rata vines, which cling on to many tree trunks, in particular, tree ferns. The most spectacular of these is the shining rata or akakura (*Metrosideros fulgens*). From February through to July, orange-red tufts of flowers appear throughout the forest. Sometimes whole tree trunks will be pillars of colour.

The native clematis, *Clematis paniculata*, heralds spring with loose festoons of large, white daisy-like flowers. This evergreen climber has a distinct juvenile phase with narrow, lobed leaves. It also carries male and female flowers on separate plants, the males being much larger and generally blooming earlier than the females. This is a plant that has adapted well to cultivated conditions. It regularly appears amongst the rhododendrons and azaleas, adding a special charm to the early season.

Supplejack (*Rhipogonum scandens*) is a climber related to the lily family. This tough plant can create an impenetrable thicket of pliable, but immensely strong stems that are difficult to cut through. All the foliage and the bright red fruit by which it spreads are way up in the treetops.

Above: The fungus Amanita muscaria, *fly agaric, which grows in conjunction with most conifers.*

Opposite: Young lancewoods striving to take their place in the bush hierarchy.

Many tree trunks are covered with a mass of leathery, sharp-edged, narrow leaves that seem to cascade down from great heights. This is kiekie (*Freycinetia baueriana* var. *banksii*), a scrambling climber (related to the screwpine family) that clings with aerial roots. It has edible male and female flowers which are surrounded by white bracts. The female fruits are fleshy and also edible, but he possums always get there first and we never see them.

Tree ferns are an important element of the rainforest, and at Pukeiti we have three common species. The most impressive is the huge, black-stemmed mamaku (*Cyathea medullaris*), which grows to 20 metres and has large fronds 5-6 metres long. It is a coloniser and quickly establishes on track margins and cuttings. Unfortunately, the possum is fond of new growth and can kill the trees. Banding with aluminium sheets is practised to keep them from climbing the trunks. This is not a problem with the soft tree fern (*Cyathea smithii*), which always has a distinctive skirt of dead fronds hanging below the flat-topped head of soft, light-green leaves. It is a common and distinctive component of the bush.

The third specimen is the wheki or harsh-leafed tree fern (*Dicksonia squarrosa*). This holds its stiff, rather rough fronds in an arching pattern, and has a clean trunk. It is the favoured species for ponga walling as the trunks are very long lasting. The trees also regrow when cut.

The silver fern (*Cyathea dealbata*) is only seen occasionally at Pukeiti, restricting itself to sunny, dry ridges, whilst the slender tree fern (*Cyathea cunninghamii*), a very tall, thin-trunked plant like a small mamaku, is found in pockets. It is common in the large-leaf rhododendron area.

Fuschia excorticata (kotukutuku) is a native tree with beautifully coloured flaking bark.

Above: A telephoto view of tree ferns in the pond area.

Right: Prince of Wales fern, (Leptopteris superba), one of New Zealand's most beautiful native ferns. It thrives in a cool, damp environment.

Ferns and epiphytic plants are special components of the Pukeiti rainforest. Without them it would not be as lush and cool, the forest floor would be open and the canopy less interesting. High humidity and mild conditions enable all sorts of plants to establish on the ground, rocks and up in trees. We always joke at Pukeiti that if you stand still for too long, something will start growing on you! Literally, that is what happens in the bush.

The perching lilies, *Astelia* and *Collospermum* species, can be found on the ground or 30 metres up in a tree canopy. Some species prefer one or the other habitats, but tolerate both. The same goes for many ferns, particularly the aspleniums. One very distinctive group of ferns are the filmy ferns, which are generally found in damp, cool situations. They usually hang off tree-fern stems and tree branches, or make a complete groundcover. These are thin-fronded ferns of a delicate nature that quickly curl up when conditions dry out. They have a wonderful translucency that is enhanced by backlighting.

Native orchids are common but, being small and often greenish in flower colour, can easily be overlooked. The scent of some, like *Earina autumnalis*, often gives them away, but finding them can be difficult. More than 12 different orchids have been recorded, and no doubt others await discovery.

Such is the makeup of the Pukeiti rainforest – a complex assemblage of hundreds of different plants, occupying many micro habitats. The forest fauna also adds to this.

New Zealand has no large indigenous land animals, and the largest birds, such as the moa, have long been extinct. Pukeiti still holds populations of geckos and lizards, though these are very hard to find. Insect life is fascinating and glow worms can be seen in some areas at night, particularly around the water-wheel. It is birds, however, that lift the spirits and enrich the forest for all to enjoy.

Kiwis have been present in the area for a very long time, but sadly that situation is rapidly coming to an end. Only 20 years ago they could be heard on most nights. Our national bird is being predated into extinction at Pukeiti by feral cats, stoats and fitches. On the positive side of the ledger, many other native birds have thrived and are present in good numbers.

Kereru, the handsome fat native pigeon, find Pukeiti and some of the exotic plantings very much to their liking. They are particularly fond of the kowhai (*Sophora tetraptera*), and all but the tips are ruthlessly decimated, to the point where one wonders how the plants survive. Only when something more tempting is on the menu do the kowhais get a respite. The bulky kereru is often heard before being seen, as it bulldozes its way through the canopy. However,

Above: Olearia cheesemanii *is a floriferous native plant with a rather pungent perfume.*

Opposite: A nikau palm seen along the walk on the way to the Hybrid Block.

visitors are often rewarded by aerial acrobatic displays which belie the bird's normal heavy-winged flight.

At the other end of the scale are the dainty fantails (piwakawaka), which effortlessly dance around visitors in all seasons bar midsummer. Their friendliness is based on 'cupboard love', for insects are disturbed by people strolling through the garden and they cash in on a free meal. Sometimes during quiet times, the dance of fantails over the main lawn is a sight to behold. To me, these gregarious little birds are the embodiment of the joys of living.

The tui and bellbird are the great garden songsters. In both cases, however, appearances can be very deceiving. Beneath the melody lies a melodrama of rivalry and one-upmanship. The tui is an aggressive bully, chasing all and sundry in its territory. A whirr of rustling wings and accompanying squawks let you know they are 'on patrol'. The bellbird in particular encounters the tui's wrath as it competes directly for the same food – nectar. Where might is right, the bellbird comes off second best. When not being unneighbourly, the tui is at home sitting high in a tree, where its iridescent black plumage glistens in the sun. The tui's repertoire of song is almost incomparable, save for the haunting voice of the kokako. The white ruff of neck feathers bob up and down when it is in full throttle, leading to its nickname of the 'parson bird'. Yes, tuis are something rather special.

The bellbird, on the other hand, is olive green with a yellow wing bar. It is a sleek, small bird of rapid flight, and well equipped to keep out of the tui's way. Apart from the tui, the bellbird will attack other birds who dare to set foot in its food tree of the moment. The bellbird's song, surprisingly powerful for a bird of its size, resonates throughout the forest. An evening or early morning session is magical, as each bird calls to the other.

Aside from the foregoing 'big four', tomtit, grey warbler, whitehead, silvereye and shining cuckoo are all present and in good numbers. Visitors may remark that there are few to see, but during the heat of the day and while they are nesting, birds retreat inside the forest. We also get visits from paradise ducks, quail, harrier hawks and welcome swallows. These join the other exotic birds that have also made Pukeiti their home. When the day-shift sleeps, the ruru or morepork (owl), stirs from daytime slumber. In the dark of the night it calls out plaintively, then looks and listens for movement.

Right: A fantail perched on a spent flax flower spike. David Medway

Opposite: The native pigeon (kereru). David Medway

Below left: A tui drinking nectar from a rhododendron flower at Pukeiti, note this rarely seen view of the tui highlights its beautiful blue wings. David Medway

Below right: A whitehead perched on a tree fern frond. David Medway

Appendix 1: Curators, caretakers and membership information

The following is a list of the curators and caretakers from 1951 to the present day. (In some instances these roles overlapped.)

Curators

Arthur Goudie, Honorary Curator 1951–3
John Goodwin, Honorary Superintendent 1953–68
Les Boisen 1954–6
Rob Bayly 1956–60
Rob Hair 1960–9
Graham Smith, Curator/Director 1969–present day

Caretakers

Les Boisen 1954–6
Rob & Claire Bayly 1956–60
Rob & Ina Hair 1960–9
Don & Nancy Lay 1969–70
Bill & Billie Plunket 1970–4
Lauri & Lawrie Cadman 1974–5
Tom & Marg Adkins 1975–6
Sol & Val Maynard–Solley 1976–8
John & Elsie King 1978–82
Owen & Joanne Barriball 1982–5
Bill & Venetia Lowe 1986–94
Peter & Karen Davis 1994–present day

Membership Information

Founder Douglas Cook is known as the Trust's Founder as it was he who bought the original block of land which got Pukeiti started.

Foundation, Founding (Sustaining) Members

These were the members (25 in total), who paid £50 a year for a minimum period of five years to get the Trust started. All persons who became Sustaining Members prior to 31.12.1951 were designated Foundation Members. Sustaining membership continued until Membership in Perpetuity (MIP) was introduced.

Associate Member

A member who paid an annual membership of £20. (Discontinued.)

Ordinary Member

A member who pays an annual membership at the standard rate of the time.

Member in Perpetuity

A member paying one major subscription for a perpetual non-transferable membership. The idea was promulgated by the late Fred Parker, and was particularly aimed at the older member, some of whom preferred this method of payment.

Life or Honorary Member

Originally, this was a member who contributed £500 in one sum, and after such contribution, paid no annual subscription; or persons who over a period of time have given outstanding service or assistance. (Rule 4(d) of the original Set of Rules, but it is believed it was never implemented.)
Today, Honorary Members are elected by other Members on recommendation of the Board for outstanding service to Pukeiti over many years.

Patron

An honorary role, elected by the annual general meeting on recommendation of the Board.

Corresponding Members

Members elected in other countries to report on subjects of interest to the Trust and who paid no subscription. (Discontinued.)

Junior Member

Designed to encourage younger family members. It was not popular, however, and has been discontinued.

Appendix 2: The walks

Through 1997 and 1998 Pukeiti is introducing new walk and track names and the new map reproduced opposite shows these revised track names and the three key walks of which these tracks are a part. The three walks have been designed to take in the three main seasonal features of the gardens at Pukeiti. Separate guide sheets will be issued for each of these walks.

Grande Way

This is an early season walk designed to take the visitor through the plantings of large leaf rhododendrons and other early-season features. The route takes the visitor through:

Cook Walk — a natural bush track linking key exotic plantings

Hybrid Block — early hybrid rhododendrons and shelter plantings

Larcom Walk — featuring magnolias, daphnes and view to the lodge

Hauler Trench Bridge — the early historical site of logging days

Giant Rata and *R. giganteum* 'Pukeiti' — two giants of their race

Valley of the Giants — a unique planting of large-leaf rhododendrons

Tunnington Bridge — view the Prince of Wales ferns below

Kynoch and Croker Walks — arboreum tree rhododendrons and *Camellia reticulata*

Lodge Lawn and Water-wheel — the first building and water supply at Pukeiti

Covered Walk — displays the superb sub-tropical Vireya rhododendron collection

Display Centre — (under the Gatehouse) for a look at the history of Pukeiti and its development.

Founders Way

This is the main season walk to view the major plantings and spring features in October and November. It takes in the:

Cook Walk — a natural bush track linking the Founders' Garden and Te Whare Taonga with the main plantings

Stead Block — an area devoted to New Zealand-raised rhododendrons

Hybrid Block — where the first rhododendron plantings were made in 1955

Ayckbourn Walk — featuring the scented rhododendron species, with a lookout to Pukeiti

Hill and Nuttallii Valley, with its imposing Himalayan species

Matthews Walk — displays of evergreen azaleas, rata tree skeletons and rare rhododendron species

Pond Lookout and Hauler Trench — view the ponds from a platform and the trench lined with yellow primulas

Azaleas and natives — evergreen azalea beds lead to a native border and rock terrace near the lodge

Lodge Lawn — the borders around the lawn are full of spring interest

Covered Walk and Perrott House — displays the superb sub-tropical Vireya rhododendron collection

Display Centre — (under the Gatehouse) for a look at the history of Pukeiti and its development.

Riverside Trail

This is a summer walk following a mountain stream and is designed to take in the natural beauty of Pukeiti's native bush. This is a more rugged walk than the grass track walks and there are some steps. The trail takes in the:

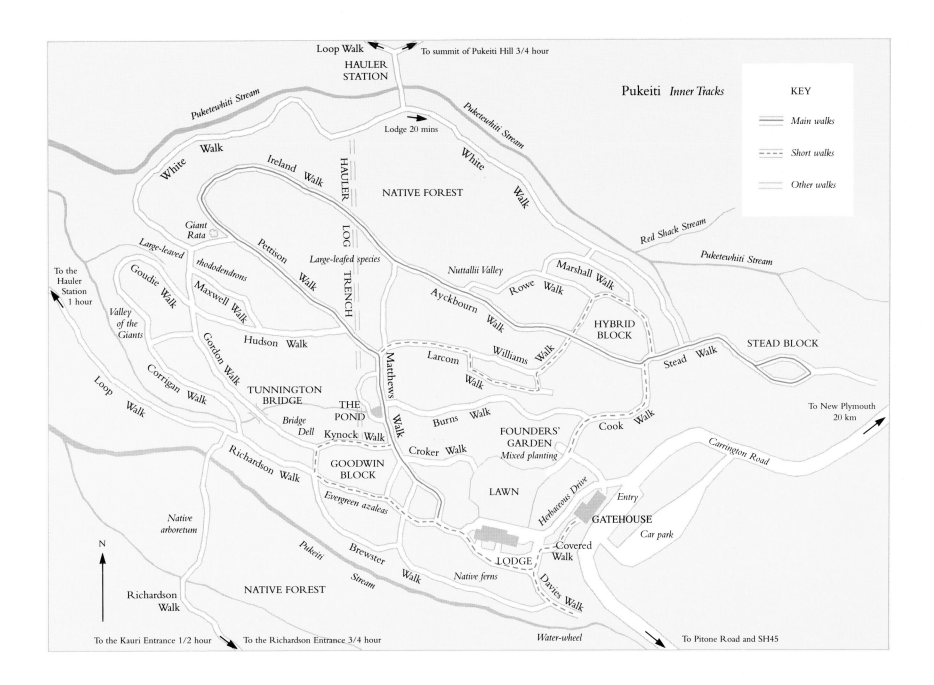

Pukeiti *Inner Tracks*

KEY

Main walks

Short walks

Other walks

Loop Walk

HAULER STATION

To summit of Pukeiti Hill 3/4 hour

Puketewhiti Stream

Lodge 20 mins

Puketewhiti Stream

White Walk

Ireland Walk

NATIVE FOREST

White Walk

Red Shack Stream

Puketewhiti Stream

To the Hauler Station 1 hour

Giant Rata

Large-leaved

rhododendrons

Pettison Walk

Large-leafed species

Marshall Walk

Goudie Walk

Maxwell Walk

HAULER LOG TRENCH

Nuttallii Valley

Rowe Walk

Ayckbourn Walk

Valley of the Giants

Hudson Walk

Williams Walk

HYBRID BLOCK

STEAD BLOCK

Gordon Walk

Larcom Walk

Corrigan Walk

TUNNINGTON BRIDGE

Matthews Walk

Stead Walk

Loop Walk

Bridge Dell

THE POND

Burns Walk

FOUNDERS' GARDEN

Cook Walk

To New Plymouth 20 km

Kynock Walk

Croker Walk

Mixed planting

Carrington Road

Richardson Walk

GOODWIN BLOCK

LAWN

Native arboretum

Evergreen azaleas

Herbaceous Drive

Entry

GATEHOUSE

Car park

N

Pukeiti Stream

Brewster Walk

Covered Walk

Richardson Walk

Native ferns

LODGE

Davies Walk

NATIVE FOREST

To the Kauri Entrance 1/2 hour

To the Richardson Entrance 3/4 hour

Water-wheel

To Pitone Road and SH45

115

Cook Walk — a natural bush tracking linking the Founders' Garden and Te Whare Taonga with Hybrid Block

White Walk — a bush walk that drops down to the Puketewhiti Stream and follows the bank before rising again to large-leaf rhododendron area

Giant Rata — view this ancient relic of years past with its hollow trunk and masses of epiphytes

Giant Lilies — at Christmas time you can see and smell these amazing white-flowered sentinels up to 4 metres tall

Tunnington Bridge — view the Prince of Wales ferns below

Brewster Walk — follow through native forest as you walk alongside the boulder-strewn Pukeiti Stream

Water-wheel — in a magnificent setting the wheel turns to provide a constant water supply for irrigation of the gardens

Covered Walk and Perrott House — see the superb sub-tropical Vireya rhododendron collection plus other tender plants

Display Centre — (under the Gatehouse) for a look at history of Pukeiti and its development.

The Founders Walks

Ayckbourn Walk

The main walk through the Hybrid Block and maddenia section rhododendrons.

Brewster Walk

A bush track featuring ferns and native plants that grow alongside the Pukeiti Stream.

Burns Walk

A short bush track along the Lodge Stream with extensive plantings of bog plants and rhododendrons.

Cook Walk

The main track linking the Founders Garden with the Hybrid Block and featuring named native plants.

Corrigan Walk

A bush track from the southern end of the Valley of the Giants that links with the Richardson Walk featuring large-leaf rhododendrons.

Croker Walk

A grassed walk from the eastern end of the Lodge Lawn with native plantings on one side and azaleas and *Camellia reticulata* on the other.

Davies Walk

This bush- and fern-lined track starts behind the lodge and leads to the water-wheel and dam.

Gordon Walk

A wide bush track from the Giant Rata to the Bridge Dell featuring large-leaf rhododendrons, giant lilies and native forest.

Goudie Walk

Track around the Valley of the Giants that looks down into the large-leaf rhododendron collection.

Hudson Walk

A new bush track providing a link between the Valley of Giants and the Hauler Trench Bridge featuring large-leaf rhododendrons.

Ireland Walk

A loop track from the Matthews Walk to the Giant Rata, stepped in parts and planted with scented rhododendron species.

Kynock Walk

This grassed track features extensive plantings of evergreen azaleas, arboreum rhododendrons, magnolias and lilies.

Larcom Walk

A grassed track through hybrid rhododendrons, magnolias and hydrangeas leading to rhododendron species near the Matthews Walk.

Marshall Walk

Stepped bush track looping between the Hybrid Walk and Nuttallii Valley with tender rhododendron plantings and Glenn Dale Azaleas.

Matthews Walk

A wide grass track through the extensive rhododendron species collection, evergreen azaleas and hydrangeas and linking many other walks together.

Maxwell Walk

A short walk through the centre of the large-leaf area featuring these rhododendrons, giant lilies, rimu and *Daphne bholua*.

Pettison Walk

This wide bush track from the Giant Rata to the Matthews Walk has major plantings of large-leaf rhododendrons and some tender species and hybrids.

Richardson Walk

A long track starting at the lodge with native and azalea borders, changing to a bush track out to the Richardson Block, half an hour away.

Rowe Walk

Bush track that links the Hybrid Block with the Nuttallii Valley and looks into the Marshall Walk valley. Vireya rhododendrons feature on a bank.

Stead Walk

A grass track leading from the Hybrid Block to the Stead Block and featuring Loderi rhodos and New Zealand-raised hybrids, camellias and hydrangeas.

White Walk

An attractive bush walk, steep and stepped in places, that follows the Puketewhiti Stream around in a loop before climbing back to the large-leaf rhododendron area.

Williams Walk

This grass walk loops around the Hybrid Block and back to the Larcom Walk and features rhododendrons, azaleas, magnolias, hydrangeas and much more.

Endnotes

Chapter 1: The founding of the garden

1 Douglas Cook, letters [1949–1953], Pukeiti Archives
2 Ibid.
3 Ibid.

Chapter 2: Pukeiti — the first 25 years

1 John (Jack) Goodwin in interviews with the author, 1995/96

2 Des Corbett in an interview with the author, 1996

3 Les Boisen, Pukeiti Rhododendron Trust Newsletter, March 1994

4 Des Corbett, op.cit.

5 Rob Bayly in an interview with Des Corbett, 1996

6 Des Corbett, op.cit

7 John (Jack) Goodwin, op.cit.

8 From Karen Williams, notes by Griff Williams, c. 1961

9 John (Jack) Goodwin, op.cit.

10 Graham Smith in an interview with the author, 1995

11 Elsie King in an interview with the author, 1995

12 Ibid.

13 Quoted from the *Daily News*, 29.10.1988

Chapter 3: Some early benefactors

1 This quote and future quotes about Arthur Richardson in this chapter from Des Corbett in an interview with the author, 1996

2 This quote and future quotes about Ned Shewry in this chapter from Des Corbett in an interview with the author, 1996

3 From article by Rob Hair in Pukeiti Rhododendron Trust Newsletter, no 35, February 1978

4 From article by Rob Hair in Pukeiti Rhododendron Trust Newsletter, no 32, April 1976

5 From article by Rob Hair in Pukeiti Rhododendron Trust Newsletter, no 35, February 1978

6 This and further comments in this chapter are from Lady Mary Matthews and Richard Matthews in an interview with the author, 1995

7 This and further comments in this chapter are from John Matthews in an interview with the author, 1996

Chapter 4: Developments (and some disasters) 1976–96

1 Des Corbett in an interview with the author, 1996

2 Quoted from *Daily News*, 1988

3 Graham Smith in an interview with the author, 1995

4 Ibid. Further comments from Graham Smith in this chapter are also from an interview with the author, 1995

Chapter 5: Pukeiti today — and tomorrow

1 This comment and further comments in this chapter from Graham Smith are from an interview with the author, 1995

2 John McIntyre, letter to the author, 1996

Bibliography

The information for this book has been drawn from the people who were involved or are still involved with Pukeiti, and from Pukeiti's own archives, including Minutes of Meetings, newsletters, letters, newspaper and magazine articles, etc. It also includes interviews and material gathered by myself, all of which have subsequently been donated to Pukeiti's archives as a permanent record. Please note that the *Taranaki Daily News* changed to the *Daily News* in the mid 1950s. The *Taranaki Herald* was a separate newspaper. It ceased operation in 1989.

A.A. Official Bulletin, February, 1953, pp. 6-7. I.M.O. re: the lead up to and the history of Pukeiti; May, 1959, pp. 20-1. I.M.O.: 'A Dream Takes Shape at Pukeiti'.

Adams, Keith, 1996, interview with the author.

Airline Review, 1968, p.13, Douglas Elliott: 'Pukeiti — Garden on a Mountain Slope'.

Bayly, Rob, 1996, interview with Mr Des Corbett on behalf of the author.

Bublitz, Lynn, 1995, conversation with the author.

Cassie, P.A. (Wendy), 1997, biographic material on Max Grant Maxwell

Clapperton, Garry (Curator), Eastwoodhill Arboretum, 1992, 1996, biographic material on Douglas Cook.

Collier, Gordon, 1996, letter to the author.

Cook, Douglas, 1949–1953, letters.

Corbett, Des, 1996, interview with the author.

Corrigan, Ross, 1996, letter providing information on his late mother, Inez Corrigan.

Cullen DSc, James (Director [? of what], 1996, letter regarding the late Stanley Smith's Horticultural Trusts

Daily News, 1976–1996, various articles.

Du Fresne, Julie, 1996, conversation with author regarding Ada Clements Kynoch.

Gardening Illustrated, February, 1954, pp.32-33, Douglas Elliott: 'A Rhododendron Reserve in New Zealand'.

Goodwin, John (Jack), 1995/96, interviews with the author.

Goudie, David, 1996, letter regarding Arthur Goudie.

Hawera Star, 11.10.1954.

Hudson, Michael, 1996, conversation with the author regarding G.B. Pettison.

Ireland, Jim, 1996, letter to the author regarding R.A. and F.A. Ireland.

King, Elsie, 1995, interview with the author.

Marshall, Roger, 1996, letter to the author regarding Alan Hadfield Marshall.

Matthews, John, 1996, interview with the author.

Matthews, Lady Mary, 1995, interview with the author.

Matthews, Richard, 1995, interview with the author.

Matthews, Russell, 1960–70, letters.

McIntyre, John, 1996, information on The House of Treasures.

Millais, J.G., 1924, *Rhododendrons and the various hybrids. Second Series*, Longmans, Green and Co, London.

Muldoon, R.D., 1980, letter regarding visit to PRT.

New Zealand Gardener, September, 1982, pp.30-31: 'Black Friday at Pukeiti'; November, 1992, p.4: 'A Curator's Story'.

North & South, August, 1996, p.116, Julie Du Fresne: 'Tree Folk'.

NZRA, 50th Jubilee Issue, 1944–1994.

NZRA Bulletin, 1968. pp.1-12; 1995, p.48, 80.

NZRA, Minutes of Meetings, 9.3.1950, 25.10.1950.

Otter, K, 1996, letter to the author regarding Pukeiti's climate range.

Pascoe, John, 1958, *The Story of Pukeiti*.

Puddle, Charles, undated, facts sheet.

PRT, 1951, Circular notice to local members.

PRT, 1953, letter regarding Russell Matthews stating his horticultural affiliations.

PRT, 1967, Executive Meeting Minutes.

PRT, 1993, *Growing Rhododendrons. A Gardener's Guide*.

PRT, Foundation Members of the Trust up to 1.11.1951.

PRT, Founders' Book, includes photographs, letters and information on most of the Foundation Members.

PRT, Minutes of the Inaugural Annual General Meeting, 31.10.1951.

PRT, Minutes of the Initial Meeting of the Board, 31.10.1951.

PRT newsletters, 1952–83.

Ragtime, 25.11.1995, pp.33-4.

Rawson, D.H., 1982, NZ Archaeological Association, Site Record Form (NZMS1). Also NZMS169, 1985, Kirihau Tram Line.

Rhododendron Festival Steering Committee, Minutes of Meeting, 1988.

Sim, Anne, 1996, letter to the author regarding R.K. and F.A. Ireland.

Smith, Graham, 1995, interview with the author.

Star, 15.6.1988, 'Pukeiti, a garden for all seasons'.

Taranaki Herald, 1954-85, various articles.

Taupo Times, 14.6.1990.

The Gardeners' Chronicle, July, 1954, p.21, 'A New Zealand Enterprise'.

The Rhododendron, June, 1976, pp.2-5, Graham Smith: 'Pukeiti — 25 years on'.

Todd, Moyra, 1967, correspondence, Pukeiti Archives.

'Uncle Joe's Garden Gossip', reprinted from the *New Zealand Home Journal*, July, 1956, 'A Rhododendron Garden for New Zealand'.

Williams, Karen, 1996, letter to the author regarding G.W.A. Williams and L.E. Williams.

Witten-Hannah, A.B., 1955, *Three Centres of Culture in Shelter of Pouakais*, Te Kotahitanga Tautoru Society.

Index